"*Soul Desires* is a m̲͟ ̲͟ ̲͟ ̲͟ portrait of the rea̲͟ ̲͟ ̲͟ ̲͟ crossroads of mental health and spirituality. Dr. Akin Merino provides an eminently practical guide to emotional health and a solid sense of self. Dr. Merino's desire to see women whole, emotionally free, and spiritually rich is apparent in this book through her warm and down-to-earth guidance."

Jeshana E Avent-Johnson, PsyD.

"This is a compelling, heartfelt read, which will challenge women everywhere to examine themselves and grow in the experience."

Dr. Elaine Walton

"This is a book that is vital for the faith-based community. It is a must read for every Christian woman!"

Pastor Ilean Frasier
Second Wind Ministries

"In *Soul Desires*, Akin passionately speaks to the heart of every woman who is not satisfied with just getting by but desires to live a dream and fulfill God's purpose for her life. She shares life-changing truths and the benefits of being connected to the true source of life and influence. The book presents truths and tools that will help readers to find true transformation in their relationship with God."

Irene Olumese
Nutrition Specialist/Writer
Geneva, Switzerland

Soul Desires

RESTORATIVE TOOLS FOR A

SOUL DESIRES

WOMAN'S SPIRIT, SOUL, AND BODY

Akin Merino, PhD

TATE PUBLISHING
AND ENTERPRISES, LLC

Soul Desires
Copyright © 2012 by Akin Merino, PhD. All rights reserved.

No part of this publication may be reproduced, stored in a retrieval system or transmitted in any way by any means, electronic, mechanical, photocopy, recording or otherwise without the prior permission of the author except as provided by USA copyright law.

Scripture quotations marked (AMP) are taken from the Amplified Bible, Copyright © 1954, 1958, 1962, 1964, 1965, 1987 by The Lockman Foundation. Used by permission.

Scripture taken from the New King James Version®. Copyright © 1982 by Thomas Nelson, Inc. Used by permission. All rights reserved.

The opinions expressed by the author are not necessarily those of Tate Publishing, LLC.

Published by Tate Publishing & Enterprises, LLC

127 E. Trade Center Terrace | Mustang, Oklahoma 73064 USA
1.888.361.9473 | www.tatepublishing.com

Tate Publishing is committed to excellence in the publishing industry. The company reflects the philosophy established by the founders, based on Psalm 68:11,

"The LORD *gave the word and great was the company of those who published it."*

Book design copyright © 2012 by Tate Publishing, LLC. All rights reserved.
Cover design by Joel Uber
Interior design by Errol Villamante

Published in the United States of America

ISBN: 978-1-62024-092-2
1. Religion, Christian Life, Women's Issues
2. Self-Help, Personal Growth, General
12.10.26

Dedication

To a company of courageous women
who choose to live their desires!

Acknowledgments

In gratitude to the Lord for love so profound and guidance so direct.

To my husband, Kevin, for being the catalyst for deeper engagement.

To my son, Lon, my joy of becoming.

To my daughters Jessica, Margaret, Abrianna, and Gabriella who make me laugh and jump into life.

To my editors who have contributed immensely to this book.

To my father, for loving us unconditionally.

Finally to all my sisters and women who are connected to my destiny, this book is for all of you.

Table of Contents

Foreword	13
Preface	15
What Is My Greatest Desire?	21
Desires Truth	25
Desires Spiritual Awakening	29
Desires Mind and Body	33
Desires to Be Recognized	43
Rachel's Cry: A Prayer	47
Rachel's Desire: A Prayer of Rededication	49
Desires Rebirth after Shadows	51
Desires a Break	59
Desires Movement	65
Desires Commitment	69
Desires to Eliminate Automatic Negative Thoughts (ANTS)	79
Desires Acceptance	89
Desires Restoration	93
Desires Intervention	97
Desires to Create a Genogram	101
Desires to Communicate	109
Desires Worship	119
Desires Forgiveness	121
Desires a Definite Word	125
Gratitude in the Dry Places	127

Declarations	132
Desires to Raise Good Children	135
Desires Abundance	143
Desires Self-Esteem	147
Desires Construct	151
Desires Faith	157
Desire to Love Yourself	159
Desires Prayers	161
Desires to Be Outside the Box	167
Desires Declarations	169
Desires Possibilities	171
Desires to Plant a Speaking Seed	174
Desires to Understand Personality Types	181
Desires *I Am*	199
Living Desires Plan	203
Define Yourself	205
Action Plan	210
The Roadblocks to Success	211
Transcendent Principles	233
Ask: What Can I Do to Help?	237
Weapons Released	239
Post Script	243
Appendix	247
References	263

Foreword

This perceptive and deeply personal book points to the disparity between the harsh realities of life and our understandings of God. Does God have a purpose for my life? Will I ever be set free from my current transgressions and sufferings? Is there hope for me? Can I be healed and restored? Dr. Merino answers these questions with clarity, richness, and biblical assurance. She takes us on a journey beyond hopelessness and disillusionment to a more profound faith and confidence in God's everlasting love. Drawing from her spiritual and psychological insights, Dr. Merino gently takes away the blinders and blazes a trail though our fears and aches to empower women from all walks of life. This book is a godsend to women yearning to reach transcendence and desiring to discover and fulfill God's ultimate purpose for their lives.

Dr. Merino is a spirit-led writer, pastor, and educator with a gift for articulating the shared experience of brokenness and the magnificent power of restoration. Her message of hope has touched the lives of countless women in her church, classrooms and community. Her previous texts, *Academic Success: Breaking the Chains of Underachievement in our Public Schools* and *Bathroom*

Therapy, exemplify her thoughtful writing style and unique ability to educate and empower those around her. Her global perspective and the integration of biblical truths and the human psyche are revolutionary. This approach adds a dimension of depth to current texts and reaches deep into the heart of the reader.

Dr. Brenda Navarrete
President/Founder
Coalition for Change

Preface

Hello ladies,

I sense that some of you are wrestling with major challenges in your life journey. The realities of the twenty-first century global recession and natural and personal upheavals are redefining paradigms. However, this is not the time to lose faith and purpose because I perceive that your tests and trial will culminate in testimonies. We can't realize the awesomeness of a mighty God without the threat of an adversary.

You are rightly positioned in your space, and your challenges are catalysts to your success. It is important for you to take ownership of your life and maintain positive declarations while reaching out to other women around you. Your restoration is tied to your ability to live your desire. Determine to finish well and do it with dignity.

Faith has wings that can propel you further than anticipated. You cannot make it with a myopic vision because faith and patience will always amplify vision. The end of a matter is better than the beginning; therefore, determine to be a woman who is transported on the wings of faith.

Shadows can never hurt you, though they loom larger than life. Troubles cast shadows on the heart's deeper quests which distract you from destiny and purpose. However, I believe that light eliminates shadows when we search for the truth in situations. Truth exists on a higher plane, and it will always illuminate.

The truth is that the Great Voice of the universe is your father, and you are a part of this great life. This universe is conspiring to favor you because the heavens are on your side. The angels are moving to align you with the deep desires of spirit, and the Son of God is engaging in prayer for your soul. You were sent here for a purpose, and all will end well with you.

It is the forgetting of our original home that makes us lose focus and wallow in the mire of self-pity and hopelessness. I am reminded of the story of the little girl who went in to her baby sister's nursery. Her mother almost froze as the she heard the little girl whisper to the baby, "Remind me of heaven, because I am starting to forget." You ate the fruits of abundance, and that is why lack is so frustrating; we were loved unconditionally, and that is why a lesser love will never suffice. You've basked in splendor, and that is why mediocrity is strange. The truth is that you are powerful beyond imagination. You can transcend your circumstances because you come from great stock! The giants who dare to face you will flee because your strength is formidable. A way of victory is ahead, and you will enter your promised land. The truth is, you are the miracle you've been praying for; you are the right woman for this moment.

This book is for women who desire to live the hidden desires of the heart and those who are spiritually or not so spiritually inclined and for the women who sit in the church pews each Sunday waiting to be rescued. This book is meant to serve as a restorative tool for all women. These are practical kingdom principles of healing and wellness that will assist in your restoration. I believe that these tools are resources for your healing and well-being. Some are spiritual, others are psychological or medical, but they are all tools for your empowerment. I especially hope that it will find its way to the women in prisons, in developing countries, penthouses, and suburban places; those in need of a voice, and those who need to find a way of out the mire.

In the book of Jeremiah, the LORD inquired about the people's pain if there was a balm in Israel. The last chapter of the book of Revelation explains that the leaves of the twelve trees were for the healing of the nations. There are healing medicines and therapies all around us, and my hope is to leave you with as many as can be located around the world.

This is your soul desire!
Akin Merino

These are the Soul Desires of:

What Is My Greatest Desire?

No one can answer that question for another. We all know what we greatly desire; however, the deepest longing of the woman is to belong. We share this great affinity for land and space; and for soul and body; a great longing for a place called home. Our spiritual desire is to be recognized and accepted by a greater presence, our *soul's desire* is to cultivate relationships, and our physical desire is to be held by the arms of another. We are relational beings, and joy is to create life within ordinary places. We bask in the wisdom of each other and cry together when we forget heaven. The women reading this book are connected by time and space in our deepest places. We yearn for the connection and glory of woman. There is glory in each one of us that seeks to manifest.

We are all seeking space and time for acceptance. We give so we can find; we travel so we can reach; we suffer with hope of tomorrow; we love with anticipation and rejoice when it is returned.

The glory of woman is in her heart, in her deepest desires, sometimes left unspoken because she has learned silence in her journey. My favorite story of redemption is that of the woman caught in the act of adultery who was dragged to the presence of Jesus. What better place to be when you have lost your dignity and grace? What better place than the presence of Jesus? This woman was accepted unconditionally, forgiven, and empowered to greatness. Her humiliation was turned into redemption. The love she sought in all the wrong places was discovered in the brokenness. I Corinthians 13 admonishes us to pursue love as the highest form of spiritual contact. Love is kind and patient; it does not keep account of evil done; it is always hopeful and rejoices when truth wins. As we seek healing through the pages of this book, endeavor to make love your set point, the reference point, and default button. The glory of woman is within her heart. We desire to live without limitations. The shamed woman in the earlier story had soul desires. No one dreams of living a defeated life.

Our earliest desires were without constraints until we realized that the world had limitations. Thus, we put our dreams on hold until moments of epiphany. Rachel, the mother of Esau and Jacob asked, after the conception of her twins, "If all is well, why am I like this?" She was doing the right things but the challenges surrounding the pregnancy caused her to search for answers. In this book, you will turn the search light of revelation on yourself and encounter moments of discomfort but do not be afraid to keep probing until the day dawns on your heart. We are purposeful creatures and we seek to make sense of our lives here on earth. *Is this what I am here for? Is there something else? Will I ever achieve the dreams in my heart?* We must begin with an understanding that everything has a purpose. The purpose of time is to give the measure of eternity. The purpose of your house key is to grant access to the house. What is your singular purpose? We should search the hidden places of the heart and ask the difficult questions like Rachel. God's Word says: "For we are God's masterpiece. He has created us anew in Christ Jesus, so we can do the good things he planned for us long ago (Ephesians 2:10)."

Desires Truth

We desire an intimate understanding of spiritual principles because we are keenly aware that there is spiritual substance around us. The Apostle Paul reminds us that, "in him we live, move and have our being" (Acts 17:28). We pray and attend church services because we want a closer relationship with the Savior or we seek meaning to a seemingly purposeless existence. For non-Christian readers, your heart bears evidence to the truth of a higher authority knowing that the acquisition of knowledge does not satisfy the quest for spirit. The distance between the human spirit and the divine is shrouded in darkness until we willingly allow the light of reconciliation to dissolve the thick layer between the two. The reconnection of the human soul back to spirit is referred to as salvation. Until your spirit is awakened, you will continue to struggle in life like a candle blowing in the wind. One of my core beliefs is that good and evil, truth and deceit are prevailing life forces; however, good and truth exist in spiritual dimensions as higher forms of reality. This should fuel our thirst for spirit instead of accepting only senses-based processes.

Human beings were to have dominion over the earth and honor their Creator through service. It was a great arrangement. This Spirit-to-spirit connection would continuously allow God to flow through us into the world outside of us. This connection enabled human beings to become arbitrators of the blessings of God to the world. However, paradise was lost, and deceit became the reality of humanity. The question of the tempter to woman "Has God said…?" became the root of rebellion against anything that cannot be perceived by the senses. Darkness is the default law on the earth; therefore, natural laws are influenced by the operation of atrophy and death. Everything in this earthly kingdom is conceived to die. We live in a physical world that requires us to depend on natural sensations in order to interpret our world; however, in order to live an authentic life, one must respond to a higher set of sensations. The hope is for women to regain dominion in all spheres of existence including spirit, mind, and body. All the systems of the earth including family, media, education, religion, politics, law, and the economy are defaulted. Each is tainted with the ego of humanity and influenced by the laws of egotism and deceit. This is why we struggle when we dance to the tune of humanism.

Our purpose as women is to give life—we are life givers. This explains why we search for ways to make life meaningful. The child who is struggling and the country in the throes of war tug at our hearts. The spirit within is asking to be recognized and afforded its rightful place. We are God's promise that restoration is possible in our lifetime. We are not simply here to take up space or engage in social discourse and religious obligations; we are here to bear witness that a woman who is spirit-led can effect change while living the life of her dreams.

> …defend the poor and fatherless;
> Do justice to the afflicted and needy.
> Deliver the poor and needy;
> Free them from the hand of the wicked.
>
> Psalm 82:3,4

It is our privilege to bring righteousness and truths into our homes and communities. Righteousness should be an ever-flowing stream in the life of a believer enabling us to meet the needs of daily engagements.

A Christian is not an ordinary human being but a person filled with the power of restoration. We get so mired in the dunghill of mundane cares that we lose the glory of our existence. You are a child of God. The offspring of a goat has its DNA; a lion cub is a lion, and an offspring of God is infused with the life of God. The Almighty calls you his child and sent you on an assignment to this place called Earth, to your particular country and home. You are not an accident of nature but a woman specially designed for her world. You came at the right time through the right parents to the right people. Before your father met your mother, you were already in the mind of God. The reason you were born on your specific date of the year is because all the resources you needed to flourish were in place. You were equipped with all the necessary tools for life.

Depression and frustration set in when we miss our way or when we do not have a thorough understanding of the seasons of life. Life becomes meaningful once you are aligned to your life source. You are an instrument of healing for yourself and those around you. You are not a liability but rather a testimony in the making. There is no one who can live your life as splendidly as you can. Lean into this truth and you will experience true transformation.

Transforming Words

- I am a woman made in the image and likeness of God.

- I hear the voice of truth today.

- I am a life source and blessing to myself, my home, and my community.

- I am in this world by design, and I move purposefully towards my destiny.

- I am aligned with Spirit.

- I today believe that I will make a difference in someone's life.

DESIRES SPIRITUAL AWAKENING

An awakening is a shift in awareness when you taste reality outside the limiting confines of the mind, and a spiritual awakening is the awakening of the soul to a higher dimension of existence. In this sphere, there is no distinction in citizenship because we all take our abode in the spirit realm. There is no higher truth than spirit because it supersedes natural laws. For example, the law of gravity is always in motion, but the law of lift, which allows a plane to fly in the air, is a higher law. The spirit realm is the transcendent dimension, and like the law of lift, the spirit allows you to live a supernatural life.

A spiritual awakening could occur without a conscious human intervention; such an occurrence is beyond the scope of human transactions. It is usually not anticipated or sought after. An "out of body" experience, a tragic accident, or being struck by lightning are a few examples of events that could precipitate spiritual awakenings. However, spiritual awakenings can also be intentional. If we set time aside in prayer and meditation, fasting and consecrations, we will be well positioned for a spiritual experience.

> For we are not wrestling with flesh and blood [contending only with physical opponents], but against the despotisms, against the powers, against [the master spirits who are] the world rulers of this present darkness, against the spirit forces of wickedness in the heavenly (supernatural) sphere.
>
> Ephesians 6:12

The young wife Hannah had a spiritual encounter after she separated herself to pray about her life problem, which at the time was infertility. Because we live in an era of medical and technological advances, we find that our first response to challenges is the acquisition of more knowledge. There is nothing amiss with seeking answers from doctors, experts, or on the Internet, but they shouldn't become our ultimate consultations. The path to spirituality is prayer. Jesus said that men should always watch and pray (Luke 21: 36). Apostle Paul echoed it with his exhortation to "pray always" (I Thessalonians 5:16). Prayer is your path to the spirit realm where all spiritual transactions are exchanged. Jesus said that which is born of spirit is spirit (John 3:6). This means that you are a spirit and have authority in the spiritual realm. Seek to use this authority in prayer. You will find that you are indeed changed, and life will be experienced in a more meaningful way. Prayer changes things and most especially, you will be changed.

Women who have engaged in prayers for themselves and their families understand that there is context in the spirit. I am convinced that diabolic determinations have been pronounced against the destinies of many, but we call them "bad luck" and walk around like lambs being led to the slaughter. The devil is your adversary, which means that he will constantly oppose the good in you. His aim is to steal, kill, and destroy you and your family. There is no negotiation with the enemy because if he can't touch you, he will try to touch everything around you. When you engage in spiritual prayers, you are exerting control over your destiny. I am always challenged by the story of Job who was called a pious and righteous man, yet decisions were being made in the courts of heaven that he was not privy to. The ramifications of that particular gathering caused him great sorrow and loss. The Christian woman is not a blip on the radar of human consciousness. You are a child of God who has been privileged to enter the secret corridors of spirit in order to align your destiny. We are encouraged in the book of Hebrew 4:16, "to come boldly to the throne of grace." If we neglect spirit, we will miss the fundamental connection to restoration. God became man to save us into the realm of spirit. Jesus's purpose for departing was to send us the Holy Spirit and "when the Spirit of truth is come, he will guide us into the truth" (John 16:13).

- I am a spirit, and I take my position in the spirit realm.

- I have no fear in me because I declare that my destiny and purpose are in congruence.

- I choose to live a magnificent life.

- I choose life, I choose God, and I choose the blessing.

- I am a winner, and miracles become my norm.

- I will accomplish my purpose.

- I am a believer, and nothing shall be impossible for me.

- No one is permitted to oppose my destiny.

- I receive faith, wisdom, and strength for today.

- I have perfect vision and clarity.

DESIRES MIND AND BODY

Freud, a theorist who is distrusted in some circles, posits that the mind consist of the ego, id, and superego. The id is the selfish mind that allows an infant to thrive. It allows the child to get the basic needs met. For example, if the child wants to eat, she cries, and she is satisfied as long as that need is met. If the child is uncomfortable, too hot or cold, or simply wants attention, the id speaks up until the need is met. The id doesn't care about anyone else's need but its own. Id likes instant gratification and can be quite inconsiderate. This is acceptable for a child, but an adult controlled by id would exhibit maladaptive behaviors. The superego is the moral self which allows us to process religion and moral beliefs. The ego is the mediator between id and superego; it allows us to satisfy personal needs without jeopardizing our moral compass. The ego should be the sensible cop, but sometimes when the ego has a difficult time mediating between both, it employs one or more of what is known as defense mechanisms.

Denial is a defense mechanism that prevents us from acknowledging the truth. You cannot handle the fact that your beloved spouse is an alcoholic, so you argue against the evidence. Displacement is when you take your anger out on a less threatening target. For example, yelling at your loved ones after an argument with your boss at work. Projection is a defense mechanism which allows you to place unacceptable impulses in yourself to someone else. The most common projection that I've encountered is when a mother dismisses her son because he reminds her of his father, her ex-husband.

Rationalization is a mechanism that allows you to save face. You rationalize that you didn't get the promotion because the boss didn't like you when the real reason was that you were not qualified. Reaction formation is taking an opposite belief because the true belief causes anxiety. You might decide to only date someone of a specific ethnic group because you find yourself biased against others.

Regression is when the ego pulls a difficult memory into your unconscious until you are ready to deal with it. Sometimes people do not remember traumatic events like abuse and trauma for self-protection. Suppression, on the other hand, is your desire to push it into the unconscious so it is not remembered. Regression is an unconscious process while suppression is conscious. Sublimation could actually determine your profession. It is acting out unacceptable impulses in a socially responsible way. This means that you could become a surgeon because of your desire to cut, a firefighter because of your obsession with fires, or sublimate your desire for danger into joining the army.

Another characteristic of the mind is its ability to store history. The mind keeps the autobiography of your life like the cross section of a Sequoia tree. The cross-sectional rings of a Sequoia tree reveal its history. The rings can tell you stories of the drought years; struck by lightning years; normal years of growth, blight, and diseased years. The entire history of the tree can be observed from this cross section. So it is with your mind. Memories that make it into your long term memory bank store your history. These are stories of loss and gain; love and hate; good and bad. These are the stories that are recorded in the player of your mind which regulates your decisions. The more powerful the stories, the stronger influence they have on your life. If your story of abandonment is the most powerful, then it will become your predominant thought, and your life will move in the direction of this singular thought. It will become the voice in your head. You will find it easier to be abandoned than to live a secure life because your player has only one track, and until it is replaced, you will perpetually hear the sound of abandonment in your mind. These stories are vital because they impact the trajectory of your life.

These significant stories become fortresses that are not easily penetrated. Forts of doubt, fear, shame, and unforgiveness cannot be penetrated or dislodged by simply reading a self-help book or wishful thinking. The mind is a powerful storyteller that can shift your perception of reality because of its connection to the amygdala, a part of the brain involved in emotional processes. The amygdala records the most fearful and intense emotions only to replay them during new engagements. For example, the amygdala captures our first experiences of love and affection, loss and trauma. If a woman's initial love experience is dysfunctional or she experienced any type of loss or cultural "isms" such as sexism, ageism, and classism, the amygdala captures these experiences and will continually signal them as prototypes. It will reject any other experiences that don't measure to these initial stimuli. These stories will significantly alter the thought pattern which will result in a damaged decision making system and ultimately change your life's perceptions. Your mind has hijacked your destiny, and the result is the propensity to mindless decisions.

Mind Decisions

- Beliefs, paradigms, commitments, and mindsets are made from primary painful encounters.

- Decisions made out of pain create deficits that must be constantly maintained.

- Mindless decisions are the strongest ammunition against your desires.

- You are unconsciously maintaining the deficits—hurt, debt, loss, lack, loneliness, etc.

Consider how difficult it would be to maintain a relationship if an unconscious mind decision was reached that you are unlovable or not deserving of love. You will adopt the victim mindset and view potential relationships as unfair contests. You might be successful in a career or vocation, but when it comes to relationships, your mind story will drive a wedge between you and your desire. You will find this particular area of your life frustrating because you seem to gravitate in the opposite direction of your desires. It will become difficult to maintain intimate relationships, and you will invariably find a way to sabotage them.

There is also the debt collector mindset. Remember the story of Cain and Abel, the brothers in the book of Genesis. Cain killed Abel out of jealousy, and the blood of Abel cried out for vengeance. When you have been egregiously wronged in life, your mind will seek to right the wrong by collecting the debt owed. Consider all the people who owe you: parents who hurt you; brothers and sisters who harassed you; friends who betrayed you; boyfriends who rejected you; pastors who failed you, and various types of inequities. You are left in a state of deficit because of spouses who promised to love but inflicted pain, who promised to stay the long haul but left you alone holding all the financial debt accumulated in the marriage. You might feel that someone owes you because you did not have a father or mother. You unconsciously determine that the world owes you because of all the injustices, and you find yourself becoming a debt collector. Somebody owes you for all the pain and suffering you've experienced in life, and you find yourself collecting debt.

You will not be able to maintain new relationships because the person will be asked to repay unknown debts. Your second husband will pay for the weaknesses of the first husband; your new friend will be put through test and trials; and your boss will recognize the chip on your shoulder. You will lose the good and end up with deficits. However, the heart is a lonely hunter, so you will end up alone unless you seek to restore your mind.

Many women suffer within the confines of churches for lack of understanding yet we cannot recognize these dysfunctions without outside assistance. The scriptures tell us that there is safety in counseling. Locate a good Christian counselor who can work with you to change these distortions. The prayers and religious observations have not alleviated the pain of unmet desires. Like the bleeding of fresh wound, the stories hemorrhage on innocent listeners until you seek healing. Mind wounds should be tended like you would a physical one. If there seems to be a dissonance between what you desire and your experiences, seek counseling.

Restoration of a distorted mindset is a miracle.

The need to share your pain with anyone who cares to listen is indicative of a wounded woman in need of restoration. Wounded soldiers who still want to remain in battle are not only casualties but will cause others to be killed if they are not removed from battle. Your maladaptive behaviors and depression will impact your children, spouse, and everyone within your circle. We never suffer alone which is why we must seek help so our loved ones can live more adjusted lives. You also need to be restored to wholeness in order to live your life.

In order to change the picture created for the woman who keeps rejecting love, one must simulate a real or imagined experience that is just as sensory rich as the prior wounding event. The goal is to eventually reload different types of experiences. I have found that natural simulations or modeling, in which you observe healthy couples in their space, can help facilitate new ways of responding which can alter the initial responses. I am also in favor of the virtual reality helmets because the brain does not differentiate between real or imagined experiences. For this woman, the virtual-reality helmet is worn which then displays a 3D experience of loving relationships. This can also be achieved through various forms of media engagement. The purpose is to immerse yourself in the reality of your intention. Your participation will help create a new paradigm for future decisions.

The spoken words of faith are restorative tools with the power to permeate the unconscious mind and help rewrite your life story. The power of the spoken word cannot be overemphasized because words paint pictures that are captured by the mind. The mind can be restored when the spoken word creates a distinct picture of your desires. The word of truth is a liberator, and you cannot be freed until you are declared free. There are no other arguments when truth is introduced. The shadow life is only relevant until the true life is declared. You are not a helpless misrepresentation but a powerfully creative spirit. You can love again. You can forgive. You can live your desires if you commit to the process. The spoken word will create new, positive, and powerful experiences to replace the wounded and painful ones.

Set some time apart to write down your innermost desires for specific troubled areas of your life. Be specific about the types of desires. For example, you want to write about what type of friend you desire to be with, including what loving and caring means to you. You want to research things that you are not yet familiar with. For example, if you are not familiar with a healthy friendship, spend some time asking questions and observing those who you admire. If you grew up in a turbulent home, you could spend some time with those who have relatively healthy homes with the understanding that there are no perfect families. Research what the scriptures say about relationships, love, and friendships. Once you have gathered enough information to start the process, begin to list the ideal friendship or relationship for you. Write the new and positive experience, not the bitter past. Write down the vision and make it clear. For example, you could write the following: "I am a good friend to Lisa, and I appreciate that she is in my life. Friendship is a gift that we bestow on those who cross our paths in life so I am blessed to share this time with her. I am my authentic self and this friendship is healing. I am free to be who I am and still be mindful of Lisa's feelings. I will graciously express and receive kindness."

Do not write: "I will try to be a good friend to Lisa. I will not let her walk over me, and I will not be bitter. I will receive kindness without bitterness." The first example expresses the organic cravings of the spirit while the second gives energy to the distorted self. By stating what you don't want, you indirectly reinforce the existing story.

> By faith we understand that the worlds were framed by the word of God so that the things that are seen were not made from things which are visible.
>
> Hebrews 11:3

DESIRES TO BE RECOGNIZED

The women of the first century were regarded as inferior to men and were mostly relegated to the duties that related to their homes. These women were considered of low intelligence, with nothing to contribute to the larger society. The rabbis of Jesus's day had little use for women. Men were not supposed to speak with women in public, even if they were with their wives, much less other women, because of public misinterpretation. This was the backdrop of Jesus Christ during his earthly ministry. His ability to reach out to women and speak to them in public was revolutionary. It seemed like Jesus was on a mission to liberate women and reintegrate them into God's family system. Jesus reached out to the outcast, the condemned, the niddah (unclean because of menstruation), and the forgotten. His mission was to free women and restore them to positions of dignity and acceptance. He allowed the *niddah* to touch the hem of his garment and released the aged Peter's mother in-law from confinement; He searched out the Samaritan outcast who had married five times and was presently living in adultery; He advocated for the adulteress caught in the sexual act; He was kissed by the condemned prostitute who bathed his feet with expensive oil; He acknowledged the gift of the generous widow who gave her last; He loved the two unmarried women of Bethany and performed his first miracle in honor of his mother.

Our uniqueness as women is the ability to hear during troubled times. The Spirit will speak to the heart especially when you have exhausted all resources. So if you are feeling discouraged, you are well positioned for a different type of conversation.

It is therefore not a surprise that Jesus was always surrounded by women who appreciated his restorative powers. They, as well as we in this century continue to seek rest. There is a strategic plan of redemption for the family of God which includes making the woman an integral part of the family. Jesus reframed the conversation to that of inclusion, that women were and are a part of the father's plan on earth.

> But then I will win her back once again. I will lead her into the desert and speak tenderly to her there.
>
> Hosea 2:14

Adam, the first man, was created to exert authority over God's creation. He started the process of naming the animals and soon found that he was completely devoid of fellowship with someone like himself. There was no one to share intimacy and partnership. Although he could converse with his God, there was an obvious lack of physical companionship. Adam stood apart in the vast acres of time, standing on the threshold of destiny without a mate. The loneliness was staggering enough to move the Creator into action.

I believe that God, the Almighty, purposely delayed the formation of Eve. He waited for Adam to realize his need for a comparable helpmate. Adam needed connection, a necessary component in personal restoration.

Adam's need for Eve was desperate enough to move the hands of the divinity. He cried and ached for her with passion so deep that it found its way to the core of creation. Woman was nursed in the heart of a man, which is why she relishes laying her head on his chest, the bastion of longing. Adam was asleep the entire time woman was created, which means that a woman's first love and devotion was to Spirit. We are unaware of how long the woman spent with her Father, but we know that God formed a beautiful being and poured destiny into her. She was alone when he made her, without distractions or disruptions. It was from the Father that the woman learned how to be loved unconditionally and how to worship. When he created Eve, the mother of all creation, she became the crowning glory of God's creation. She was the essence of God's nature and man's soul. The father put Adam in a deep sleep so He could knit Himself into her destiny code. He made sure that there would always be a place for Spirit in her life. He spent time creating the mother of humanity whom He loved deeply. God presented his daughter, Eve, to Adam in the first marriage performed on earth. The marriage was beautiful and her splendor blinding. She was the ultimate gift from God to her husband.

Eve was a participant in her husband's act of high treason, because Adam violently turned against God in the greatest act of rebellion and betrayal. This single act was so unwarranted and malicious that it changed the course of history. In an act of solidarity, they both chose material over spirit. Eve crossed the threshold of innocence into the pathos of hard work and struggle, "your desire shall be for your husband and he shall rule over you" (Genesis 3:16). This precipitated the pursuit of love and loss; lust and envy; jealousy and revenge; ever seeking and never finding the peace or the man who will satisfy the soul.

As Jesus traveled the streets of Palestine, he was provoked by the mistreatment of women. He witnessed women dragged to be condemned; voices stifled and glory diminished. Jesus agonized over the experiences of women during his time, and he took the time to make contact with these daughters of God.

Jesus set out to court them; to lure them out of their hiding places; to publicly honor them and reveal the purpose of their existence. His message to all these women was simple:

> …Because the LORD has anointed me, to bring good news to the afflicted; He has sent me to bind up the brokenhearted, to proclaim liberty to captives and freedom to prisoners…
>
> Isaiah 61:1

Rachel's Cry: A Prayer

Where have I gone wrong?
When did I replace knowing him with serving him?
My heart has turned away from the beating heart
 of the Savior. I have lost my way. Will I
 recognize you today?
Who is this God we serve in the 21st Century?
An era of relativism and social reasoning;
Protestant Manipulation; Catholic pontification;
 Evangelical Exploitation and Pentecostal
 Exaggeration
Spiritual shallowness always pants for judgment
 and vengeance

Father! Father! Can you hear my cry?
Your daughters have lost their way
I ask for mercy and hope today
To return to the place of truth and grace
May our hearts seek the deepest places in you
Deliver us from self preservation
Our wounds and hurts have forged the gorge of
Selfishness which moves us away

(Merino, 2011)

Rachel's Desire: A Prayer of Rededication

Father! Father! We long to see your face
As you search our inward places
Remind us of imperfections you consider friends
Free us from self; deliver us from suffering
Set us free from anguish of defeats
Reveal yourself once again in our Land, O Lord.

Saturate us with desire for you
Like Jeremiah, let your Word burn like fire
Like Peter, ask us again if we are consumed
    by your Love
Let our hearts burn with passion for you.
Teach our hearts to ache in pursuit of Love
Forgiveness instead of Revenge
Obedience wins over Sacrifice.

(Merino, 2010)

Desires Rebirth after Shadows

> I am the resurrection and the life.
>
> John 11:25

The focus of this chapter is the rebirth after a cessation of life. A rebirth happens during times of turbulence, when we walk through the valley of the shadow of death but end up on the other side with a sense of victory. We all experience death as the loss of power in certain areas of life. Sometimes it is a failing marriage, a child lying in the hospital, lost dreams and desires. These shadows are supposed to be temporary states; however, since systems resist change, most of us accept shadows as the norm. We are comfortable, so we adapt our lifestyle to the lesser. Shadows are powerful forces that prevent people from embracing life. These shadows include engagements with loneliness, loss, sickness, and lack. It is comfortable to live in the dissatisfaction of a false reality that allows us to live the life of least resistance. For example, a woman who was betrayed by her friend decides to avoid close relationships. She struggles with the pain of betrayal but decides to shield herself from future pain through isolation. Loss can become so stressful that some women avoid investing too much in life. This woman lives in the shadow of true friendship. The death of the relationship must be acknowledged and the pain triaged in order to live an authentic life. The company of women reading this book must recognize that shadows allow us to experience the other side of happiness. It is in experiencing pain that healing is appreciated. We can't live in pain for the rest of our lives. Women who are in troubled relationships, locked up in prisons, or have lost loved ones or material possessions can identify with this concept of shadow living. We pretend to be in perfect marriages, to love life, to be great ministers of the gospel while the reality of our existence is under the shadow of death. The reality is that we are alone and scared.

Rebecca was thrust into the shadows after the death of her husband of fourteen years. Since her husband handled all the finances while she stayed home with the young children, she didn't realize that they were in financial troubles. After the sudden death of her husband from a heart attack, she also lost the home and business they had worked for the past decade. He had mismanaged the finances and made bad investment choices, and they owed several people and banks money. Rebecca had to file for bankruptcy, but she finally decided to get a law degree while her mother helped her with the children. She asked God to help her forgive the past so she could move on. Ten years later, Rebecca is successful attorney with wonderful children, but she cannot bring herself to completely trust any man. Rebecca, who still lives in the shadow, needs a rebirth for a balanced life.

Rebirth is when we flourish or increase after a decline. It is the ability to emerge from shadow places. One of the catalysts of a rebirth is relationships. I believe that we heal through the relationships in our lives. While dysfunctional relationships have the ability to destroy life, healthy relationships are innately restorative. The scripture emphasizes that we are the carriers of the life of God. This means that we are healing vessels and carriers of grace and mercy. It is in the context of relationships that we learn forgiveness, longsuffering, and trust. Jesus could speak to the dead Lazarus with such passion because he was connected intimately to him. A woman who has lost a friend needs to become a friend to another; healing occurs through connections. A young lady who was verbally abused will be restored when she connects with someone who verbally encourages her. Who are the connections in your life? We emerge from the shadow to the sacred when we come in contact with people who grace our lives with their healing balm.

Another very important catalyst in a rebirth is the belief system. Jesus emphasized this particular point to Martha, that all things are possible to believers. You can't experience life until you believe in its possibility. You can't argue with someone with a strong belief system. Believing is trust that your life is moving in the direction of purpose. Belief is also of the heart. In order to experience those soul desires, one must venture out of the limitations of the senses. Sometimes you simply must believe that the universe is working in your favor. It was expected that Lazarus had breathed his last. It was expected that the crowd of five thousand who gathered to hear Jesus would be sent away hungry or have to fend for themselves. Human beings only think within the sphere of their experiences —that which is known as schema. Schema is the framework created by past experiences, through which I interpret new information. Experience dictates that life after bankruptcy is difficult especially if you are a widow with two children. However, hope is the belief that things change and that a rebirth is possible. Rebecca believed that she could resurrect her financial life which she did with help of her family; however she needs the same belief catalyst for her relationship. There are no limits to the possibilities of your life when you dare to believe. Is it possible for the dead to rise again? It was not in Martha's schema that the dead should rise in this life until she met Jesus. I am not sure what you are going through at this moment in your life that looks absolutely impossible but I challenge you to believe again. Your mind can only interpret new information based on the old data, so it becomes imperative to reload a new program for your restoration. You can see again. You can dance again. You can be happy again. You can enjoy life again. You can become who you were destined to be again. Life can be better now. What are the steps required in the belief process?

- Pray.

- Create a new thought.
- See yourself in this new reality.
- Commit to this new process.
- Make decisions that move you in the direction of your new reality.

> For assuredly, I say to you, whoever says to this mountain, 'Be removed and be cast into the sea,' and does not doubt in his heart, but believes that those things he says will be done, he will have whatever he says.
>
> Mark 11:23 NKJV

Another catalyst for rebirth experience is meaningful words. Words are like seeds that transport life. They will grow if they are released into the proper environment. The words that you speak have the power to change your life and could make the difference between where you are and where you want to be. Words create the filter through which you perceive your world. For example, if you say the word, "lonely," you will immediately have a picture of someone who is not connected to another. Words paint pictures. The challenge is that we use words to communicate our hurts to others instead of using words as medicine. Instead of "lonely," try other words like attractive, loved, friends. When you begin to say how friendly and loved you are, you will start thinking about people acting lovingly towards you and as you think it, you will speak in congruence with your thought until you will begin to experience a self-fulfilled prophecy. Words influence your thoughts which in turn influence your actions and move your life in the direction of soul desires. This means that you are one thought away from a transformation. You do not have to settle for a mediocre existence. You do not have to settle for someone else's version of life. It is time to reorganize your life by speaking your soul desires. Dysfunction is part of the old schema; functional is the new schema. Lack is an old paradigm; prosperity is the new way. Speak!

Some women have experienced the dark night of the soul caused by injustices perpetrated by those who were supposed to care about them. Some of you are not serving God today because you've been hurt by someone in a position of authority at church. You trusted them only to realize that they were not really on your side. It is time to understand that religious leaders are sometimes wounded healers who are in need of healing themselves. Wounded healers only minister from a position of pain. Those who minister from this position are bound to hurt you. The good news is that you can be restored. The story of the woman with the issue of blood is analogous to this situation because she had been isolated by the very people who should care for her soul. The religious leaders and their rules had isolated her. However, her 'trail of tears' was intensified by the determination to see Jesus. Christianity is more than a religious affiliation; it is a relationship. We are called to take a journey with the Lord of the universe. Although people coming alongside us during the journey might cause us pain, we must not forget the ultimate reason was the primary relationship. Like the woman with the issue of blood, we can only set ourselves free from the condemnation and isolation by moving towards truth. Your move might be slow at first, but you will gain speed as you go. Decide to walk in the light that you have and your life will become illuminated. Slowly but surely, you are setting yourself free from the past wounds.

- Rebirth is experienced through the power of Spirit.

- It is the same power that raised Jesus from the dead.

- It is the power that sets the captive free.

- It is the power that created the heavens and the earth.

- It is the power that formed life on the inside of a virgin named Mary.

- It is the power that transformed fishermen into great men.

- It is the power that turned a group of 120 people into billions of followers.

- It is the power of the Creator. It is the power of Love. Do you believe?

Desires a Break

The *break* is that moment in time when you are given the opportunity to shine. It is when you defy expectation by entering the flow of your talents and skills. It is the time when all the hard work pays off. The song line, "Give me one moment in time when I feel eternity," speaks to the concept of the human heart waiting for a break. The *break* is around you at all times. As you flow with the Spirit and remain within your circle of favor, develop your gifts and talents, the *break* will be revealed when you are ready. The Chinese proverb says that the teacher will appear when the student is ready. Another term for this concept is opportunity.

No outside force determines your *break* because choices in life determine the opportune time.

Life is a series of choices, but most of us shadowbox through life. We are constantly fighting and worrying, wrestling against our own nature. Anxiety and worry are more familiar to us than peace and tranquility. A tree does not struggle with its identity. It takes its place in the dirt and grows up in wonderful manifestation. Irrespective of the elements, rain or shine, a tree never ceases to take its place. The river flows; a bird flies; fish swim, and a woman should flourish in her own skin.

Take your place. Flourish! You are magnificent; you are supposed to succeed. Arise and shine. It has been said that success is when preparation meets opportunity. If we keep perfecting our skills and talents, we will eventually be extraordinary. That is the break we desire. Your gifts will always create your life's song. Resuscitate your gifts and talents so you can live purposeful lives.

The God who rested on the seventh day still seeks rest for his people. God is at peace, and a restless soul is devoid of Him. In peace is your prosperity. We do not prosper during chaos or war. Struggles and conflict are not conducive environments for prosperity. Nelson Mandela's struggle took him to prison, and it was there that he learned peace. It was the peace that led him to the presidency. King David desired to build a magnificent temple for his God but he had lived as a man of war all his life. His son Solomon would later build the temple in the times of peace. Your growth is stunted during times of negative engagements, and most of you have turned your homes and hearts into war zones. Because your hearts and homes are filled with the anger, angst, bitterness, and regret, you repel the very things that you desire.

There are women who hate their lives and secretly desire a *break*. We hear statements like, "When will it be my turn?" "When do I get a break?' I have news for you: you are the arbiter of your opportunities. We determine when we are ready for provisions in life. We take ownership of our destiny when we enhance benefits and reduce risks. There is no woman who has only benefits or all risks. We all fall somewhere in the center. We succeed by enhancing the talents and gifts and limiting weaknesses. When we concentrate on the risks, we fall into the war zone; but if our focus is on the benefits, we position ourselves to receive more benefits. The theory of optimum performance in sports psychology includes the concept of the flow; this involves a state in which there is congruence between the perceived demands of an activity and the abilities of the performer. During flow, a performer loses self-consciousness and becomes completely immersed in the task at hand. This is the moment when the athlete is at his best. We all desire that moment, and according to sport psychologists, flow is a needed requirement for that particular breakthrough.

Several interventions are suggested to achieve the flow. Centering helps to calm athletes and get them focused at critical moments during their sport. Centering will work for the woman who needs to focus on her success. This technique requires you to focus your attention on the center of your body, the area just behind your naval button. Centering has a calming and controlling effect, providing an effective way to manage anxiety. You are required to stand with your feet shoulder-width apart, arms hanging loosely by your side. Close your eyes and breath evenly, trying to keep the tension in the upper body to a minimum as you breath. Inhale deeply from your abdomen (your stomach will extend) and be aware of the tension in your face, neck, shoulders, and chest. As you exhale, let the tension fall away and focus on the feeling of heaviness in your stomach. Continue to breathe evenly and deeply and focus your attention on the center of your body, the area just behind your naval button. Maintain your attention on that spot and continue to breath evenly and deeply, feeling controlled, heavy and calm. As you breathe out, think of a word that encapsulates the physical feeling and mental focus you want, like "relax" or "calm."

Creating a mental blueprint for success is one of the best ways in which to enter the zone. Athletes are encouraged to practice key aspects of their sport in their mind's eye both prior to competition and, given the opportunity, during breaks in competition. The scriptures admonish us that, "As a man thinks, so he is" (Proverbs 23:7). We are only one thought away from the next breakthrough. Women should also spend the time creating blueprints for success in their mind's eye. See it on the inside by immersing yourself in the senses of what your success looks like.

Parking an error is a way by which the error can be forgotten to enable athletes to focus on the here and now. The Apostle Paul stated that the key to his success was the ability to forget the past including the errors of yesterday. Parking an error is to make a conscious gesture to acknowledge the error while not owning it. This can be done by throwing a penny in a jar and moving on to the next practice instead of getting caught up in your mistakes and allowing a collapse in strength.

Losing self-consciousness is an important technique for women who are determined to achieve their soul desires. Many sports people report that they become very distracted by the presence of spectators, officials, and other competitors. The anxiety provoked by onlookers at competitions is induced by a natural fear of evaluation. Some competitors are able to turn this to their advantage, while others are completely debilitated by it. The use of self-affirmation statements will reinforce the required positive mindset. For example, "No one can resist my good" or "I am overcoming every obstacle in my life."

Simulated practice helps athletes by once again creating a mental blueprint for how to react in particular situations. For example, it might be important to create a mental blueprint of your vision. Blueprints are very specific so describe how you see yourself, including smells, taste, colors and energy, what you see yourself wearing, your conversations, and the setting where it all happened.

Athletes are asked to think about the winning feeling by bringing to mind their most successful performance ever. They are encouraged to remember this specific performance in detail so they can recreate it at will. The winning feeling is important to win. What women can learn from this technique is to remember the time that you were exceptional and recall that feeling because it will help you jump the bridge to success. In those cases where you can't seem to recall success, I want you to ask the miracle question, "What will my life be like if I had no limitations?" I want you to talk about your miracle life, and you will get that winning feeling.

Finally, the power of sound cannot be overemphasized. Music has the ability to bring you to a relaxed state. We are told in the book of Revelation that heaven is saturated with sounds of praise and worship. We also understand that heaven is a place of abundance, peace, and love; therefore, if you want to bring these qualities into your life, it is important for you to saturate your atmosphere with powerful music.

DESIRES MOVEMENT

> God told Abram: "Leave your country, your family, and your father's home for a land that I will show you.
>
> Genesis 12:1

Movement is the first step to breakthrough. Don't wait until everything is perfect to move forward. Take initiative. Do what other people are not doing. Keep moving toward purpose. Abraham would never have obtained the blessing in his father's house without taking that first step into the unknown.

Movement builds momentum, which leads straight to the path of breakthrough. It was the steps taken by Sojourner Truth and the abolitionists that started a movement which changed the destiny of a nation.

Movement is the elixir for fear. It creates the energy that silences the pangs of fear and ambivalence. We must begin to step into destiny by taking the next best known step. It could be as simple as completing an application; writing a few words on paper; a bowl of soup for the homeless. It is not saving the world but it is making a difference in one person's world.

Movement opens the door to opportunities. Benjamin Franklin said that "…to succeed, jump as quickly at opportunities as you do conclusions." People who take initiative and work hard may succeed or may fail, but anyone who doesn't take initiative is guaranteed never to succeed. Jesus said, "I will do the work of him who sent me while it is day, for the night comes when no man can work" (John 9:4).

Movement provides the energy needed for your progress. You cannot refer to yourself as a failure, even though you might have failed several times, because failure is a state of being. However, your state of being is success. The scriptures encourage us to give thanks to the Lord who always causes us to triumph. An overcomer who failed simply needs to try again until she succeeds. Your natural inclination is to flourish, and it is now time to take the necessary steps to actualize your soul desires. Move toward peace and decide that you will fulfill your purpose. Why peace? The word peace in the Hebrew language means "nothing broken and nothing missing." Peace is therefore the perfect state of human success. What does this mean for the woman who has limited resources and does not see any way out of her predicament? She should strive towards peace and move away from chaos and war. It is easy to remain in the place of struggle and pain, to live in the shadow land, but healing comes when we move towards peace. You cannot achieve the soul desires until you move.

Movement includes having a strategy and executing the plan. If you need to lose forty pounds, the strategy must include losing the first pound. We must keep moving like the woman who kept pressing her way to Jesus. She didn't allow the naysayers to distract her from her plan. The same must be said of us; let's keep the priority sacred and not be distracted by extrinsic stimuli. If you are a woman from a developing country reading this book, remember that these principles are universal. If you put the strategies in this book to work, you will reap the same results. The lack of resources or opportunities in your countries does not render these principles ineffective. Remember that the blessing is upon you, which means that you will create opportunities. You can produce an oasis in the desert. The power within you is not determined by geographic boundaries. Every believing woman has the propensity to succeed.

When you lack the energy to get out of bed in the morning or the thoughts are becoming too heavy to carry alone, I ask you to climb out anyway, or crawl if you have to, but do not lay there. Call a minister, friend, or therapist. Find a way out of the financial devastation. Send out another resume; call your debtors and explain your situation with a determined effort to pay back; read a book or even better yet volunteer to read a book to someone else. Dance, sing, praise! But do not remain in one place. Movement creates the change needed to move you to the next phase of your life. If Abraham had stayed in Horeb, there wouldn't be a nation of Israel. If Joseph had stayed in Potiphar's house, he wouldn't have become the prime minister. If Esther did not move toward the king to seek pardon, there would be no nation of Israel. If Jesus had not taken the steps toward the cross, there wouldn't be salvation for the world.

Take a step of faith toward your future. Small beginnings are befitting as long as we keep the momentum. Whatever your heart is telling you to do is worth pursuing. We are all one thought away from the next level of success. If you can think it, you can move toward it. Make a call. Visit a museum. Write a book or an article; bake a cake—nothing is too small to grow. Faith as small as a grain of mustard seed will move mountains. Your relationships will flourish if you do not give up. You will have joy again. Your heart will heal, and tomorrow will be a better day. If you plant, things will grow. Your joy will eventually overtake sorrow, your seed will overtake drought, your love will overtake apathy, and your faith overcomes the world.

> LORD, grant me the strength to keep moving even when my failures weigh me down. I will move forward, and I will not fail. I will not struggle with my existence. I belong here, and I will prosper in this land, just like a fish flourishes in the ocean. I move away from confusion and anger; I let go of anxiety and bitterness and move toward peace, joy, and prosperity.

Desires Commitment

God wants to work through his women. He wants his women to take ownership of all that has been put in their care. Commitment is a misunderstood concept because we speak of being committed to something when in fact we are not. Commitment is what we spend our energy and resources pursuing. A woman might say that she is committed to her children or spouse but spends most of her time, energy, and resources doing other things. She is committed to the latter, not the former. There are several levels of commitments which should determine our priorities. God should be the first commitment, followed by spouse, and then children followed by other relationships. We get in trouble when we get this hierarchy out of order. God, who should be our highest commitment, has asked to be first. Putting God first allows all the other relationships to work. I have seen that life does not work quite right if we are out of order.

Higher purpose is the call to the mountaintop. It is recognizing that there is something of greater importance than the self. Higher purpose is committing to something greater than us. It is accepting that you are a part of the intricate design of God. Women are created to do great exploits for God. The things that God has revealed in your hearts are important to him. Women were the last of his creation for a purpose. We are his finishing touches, the crowning glory of his creation. He wants to show us off to the world like never before as we commit to his higher purpose.

Why is it that some people are successful and others never attain their goals? Sometimes they don't even have goals. What's the secret that pushes some over the top while others never even begin the climb? There are probably many reasons—maybe low self-esteem, a negative attitude, and unbelief, to name a few. But I think the largest obstacle between us and higher purpose is a lack of total commitment. Oftentimes we say things like, "Well, I'll try. I guess I could. I hope I can." But I want to tell you that's not commitment. Commitment is simply two words, totaling five letters: Commitment is *I will*. Commitment is *I am*. My struggles and experiences over the years have proven without a doubt that commitment gets the job done. That's what separates the achievers from the sustainers. Commitment to higher purpose means that we are living out the scriptures in everyday life. Apostle Paul referred to his converts as living epistles that were read by men. God calls us witnesses to the world, and I like to refer to us as living proofs. We are living proofs that there is a higher power and higher order of existence. Many might never read the scriptures on love and grace, but we should be committed to manifesting these concepts on a daily basis.

Commitment is a dynamic force that all human beings possess. How many of us work with someone who constantly complains about her workload and promises she won't take on another project and then does? She may say she's committed to balancing her life, but if what she's really committed to is proving that she's the hardest working camper, she'll continue to over-commit and over-extend. Our actions demonstrate our commitment. Commitment is not what we say; it is what we do. Commitment begins an adventure. It is the backbone and driving force of achievement. Commitment is the triumph of possibility over all the reasons why "it can't be done," of creation over mere change. Commitment and the power of your word set new worlds into motion.

Commitment dictates the events that we allow into our lives. Commitment emanates from the deeper recesses of our soul realm and in turn demands actions. Whether you know it or not, you're honoring past commitments. It could be as primal as trying to keep a relationship alive even though we already made a prior commitment to not being trapped by someone else's limitation. We will eventually sabotage the relationship no matter how hard we think we're trying to sustain it. It could also be as spiritual as: I want to serve the LORD but can't ever seem to get closer to God because I made a commitment never to get close to any man. Since God is seen as a paternal figure, we stumble at forming bonds with him.

Commitment has long-term power. Most of our commitments are formed by the time we reach adolescence. Most of us spend the rest of our lives honoring commitments that were formed based upon actions of others including parents, siblings, relatives, close friends, teachers, and others.

The only thing that can change a prior commitment is a higher commitment to something more important than your present state. Making a spiritual commitment is always life changing and central to core beliefs. Commitment to spiritual awakening will melt the heart's wax. This type of commitment culminates in new habits like community building, spiritual awakening, and self-care. There are other types of powerful commitments that resonate deeply, including a decision to adopt a child, assist someone else in need, and any projects that are for the greater good of humanity.

Since commitments have consequences in the realm of action, our actions should manifest peace and purpose.

Mary the Mother of Jesus Was Committed

Mary the mother of Jesus was committed to the higher good. She was humble enough, tenacious, and committed enough to permit her body to become the channel through which the Savior was transported into this world. Most Jewish girls of her era anticipated that the Messiah would be conceived by a virgin from the line of David as declared by the prophet Isaiah.

Mary, like a lot of young girls her age, was committed to becoming the virgin who would conceive the Messiah. When God favored Mary above the other girls, she received confirmation through the angel Gabriel that the power of the Holy Spirit would aid in this miraculous occurrence. Mary asked the most pertinent question, "How can this be since I have not known a man?" This pertinent question is asked when reality and faith are misaligned. We ask how this can be when our present interactions and call to a higher level of faith are incongruent. It is usually a search for clarity. Yet we are aware that this higher-level question is a spiritual search for meaning. Her commitment to the birth of Christ was demonstrated in asking the right question.

When there is a cognitive dissonance, we are uncomfortable. Cognitive dissonance is when you hold two conflicting thoughts. Mary, like any of the young girls her age, knew that a virgin would have a baby. She also knew that a woman could not get pregnant without the insemination of a man. This is why she asked the question. Dialogue is initiated when the reality of your present belief system conflicts with another incoming belief. For those of us who have dared to dream higher purpose, we ask, "How can this be??" How can I speak in front of people when I'm so shy? How can I bring my broken family together when…?" We can all complete our, "How can this be? How can we fulfill our commitments with all these mitigating circumstances?"

The answer from the angel was that Mary would receive divine assistance. There is divine enablement available to women. Supernatural sense begins where common sense stops. Commitment is the ability to stay the course. It is staying power which permits us to complete those things that were started. It will allow you to fulfill your desires, stay in your marriage, and to keep searching for solutions. Commitment takes you the long haul. Mary was a young Jewish girl who was committed to higher purpose, and she ended up changing the world. What is the highest commitment of your life? If anything takes priority over spiritual commitment, life will be a series of frustrations.

Mary the Sister of Martha and Lazarus Was Committed

The second Mary is the other sister you hear preachers extol. She was the perfect sister, the one most of us love from a distance. She is a representation of what can be achieved when we commit to seeking higher purpose. Mary was at the feet of Jesus all three times we met her. Mary's relationship with Jesus changed the trajectory of her life which culminated in her anointing him.

Days before his death, Mary understood that the master, her friend, would soon be put to death. Although Jesus had talked to his disciples about his death, they didn't seem to grasp the imminent event. But this woman got it! The significance was lost to everyone at that super table but Jesus and Mary. The courage to accomplish her mission was based upon her commitment to Jesus. She defied all tradition by making herself known in the presence of men. Imagine if you will, Mary pulling back her chair ever so gently and rising with her box of alabaster in her hands. All eyes are on Mary now. She has taken the first step, and every single nerve in her body is screaming for her to sit down. She feels Martha beckoning her to sit, not to embarrass the family. Lazarus is intently focused on his sister who is taking the master's attention off him. All the stares were accusatory, and she knew everyone especially her sister, Martha, wanted the focus on the "just risen" Lazarus. She was destabilizing the status quo, and everyone except Jesus wanted her silenced. In her mind, she responded to Martha, her sister.

MARY'S MONOLOGUE

There is a reason why I can't turn back now. You see, I remember those painful nights before the master walked into my life. The shame of not having a husband and the agony of losing the sole family provider and brother is excruciatingly humbling. Martha, I spent time with Rabbi Jesus because I was going crazy. My world was falling apart, and I needed someone to lift me out of the depth of despair. It wasn't that I didn't want to serve with you, Martha. It was that my commitment to Him has consequences in the realm of action. I apologize for embarrassing you, but I have to anoint his feet and worship one last time. You see, he's sitting right there, the one who changed my life and gave me purpose. What I am about to do pales in comparison to what I've received from him.

Mary once again finds herself at the master's feet. She uncovers the box of expensive perfume and poured it on his feet. The whole house fills with the aroma of her love for the master. As she unties her hair (another break from tradition) to wipe the master's feet, Mary completes her greatest act of commitment. If you would like to know what I'm committed to, observe present preoccupation. Mary was always preoccupied with Jesus.

As Jesus staggered through the streets of Jerusalem with the hatred of men unleashed at him, as drops of blood paved De la Rosa, Mary's perfume rose up as a sweet-smelling aroma. Every time he caught a whiff of that perfume, he remembered Mary's commitment, and it gave him the encouragement to keep moving in the direction of the cross.

So there, we have the tales of two women. The first Mary was committed to his birth while the other was committed to his burial. Two women who were committed to higher purpose realized their greatest work. They stripped themselves of self-consciousness and self confidence which are the enemies of commitment.

My prayer is that we renew our commitments to higher purpose. God's higher purpose for his women is to manifest the desires of His heart. Let us take a minute to pray that this season finds us closer to the

Father. It is only when we draw close to him that we receive strength to change.

DECLARATIONS

I am a giver. My loving God deserves my loving self.
There is no obstacle between me and the spirit;
>I give myself freely to worship.

I am committed to God.
I am committed to self.
I am committed to family.
I am committed to friends.
I am committed to community.
I am committed to my world.

Four Connections of Commitment:

- To visualize

- To become persuaded

- To embrace

- To confess

Write your commitment. The book of Habakkuk admonishes us to write the vision and make it clear.

When our innermost desire finds its satisfaction in God, we will not be racing around for other thrills. We will not be driven by money, or career success, or public opinions. The commitments we make to our families will flow from our desire to honor God and do what he says. The commitments we make to the church will be made within that framework of obedience and worship of God. The financial commitments we make will serve God. Life will have a stable order and structure to it because it will have the right foundation.

Commitment to higher purpose proceeds from a heart that is fully persuaded to stay the course. If you are on the wrong path in life, make a determination to go in a different direction. It's been said that the definition of foolishness is doing the same things and expecting different results. Determine to make a shift to a higher purpose.

Desires to Eliminate Automatic Negative Thoughts (ANTS)

Aaron Beck is the developer of cognitive therapy, a type of psychotherapy that focuses on the effect of thought patterns on behavior. If I believe something to be true, I will begin to see life through that particular prism, which in turn affects the way I feel and the experienced outcomes. Depression is correlated to the automatic negative thoughts that are experienced by women. If you think something to be true, you will start to believe it, which leads to a self-fulfilling prophecy. If I believe that somebody does not like me, then I will start behaving in such a way that the person won't like me to justify my belief system. We must change these faulty patterns in order to live a satisfying life. The Apostle Paul admonished the Roman church to change their lives by renewing their minds. The strongholds in the mind will cause you to live a defeated life. It is sometimes more dangerous than the perceived evil forces on earth. "…let God transform you into a new person by changing the way you think" (Romans 12:2).

These scriptures explain the powerful impact the mind has over the quality of your life. While it is important to pray, fast, and worship, it is almost as important to become aware of your mind. Mind your mind! Become aware of the thoughts and the stories you tell yourself about your life because they eventually manifest as your life stories. Cognitive therapy is directed at distortions or faulty thought patterns, which end up becoming drivers of your life experiences. Here are some examples.

All-or-Nothing Thinking: Jane recently hurt her friend's feeling by referring to a sensitive topic during a conversation, and she now feels that the relationship is over because she is insensitive. She concludes that she cannot develop close friendships.

All-or-Nothing Statements: "I am not good enough." "It is all my fault." "Everyone is against me."

This type of thinking is characterized by absolute terms like always, never, and forever. Few situations are ever absolute, and these statements are not based upon truth. Truth is defined as the highest form of reality in existence. What is the truth in this situation? You cannot always be a failure, and everyone cannot all be against you. Why? Because you have goodness in you, and we all have tendencies to certain faults. Just because one thing did not go right does not mean that all things are wrong. The truth is, all things will work in your favor. No matter how many times you fail, you are not a failure. Everyone is not against you, and you are not damaged goods. You will rise again. You will love again. You will work again. It might not have worked out this particular time, but you will get another chance. That is truth according to scripture.

Jane should remind herself that developing friendships involves getting hurt on both sides, but it is richly rewarding.

Counseling is always the next best step if Jane finds herself unable to change these thoughts.

Overgeneralization: Tamara is lonely and often spends most of her time at home. Women from her church women's group sometimes ask her to join the activities. She feels that it is useless to try to meet people. No one really could like her. People are all mean and superficial anyway.

When one over-generalizes, one takes an isolated case or cases and assumes that all others are the same. Are people really all mean and superficial and could never like her? What about the women in the church group who are trying to get her to participate in activities? It is obvious that there are people who have taken interest in her and who care enough to want to include her in their space. Tamara's story might have been conceived from a past experience where she was hurt by a church group or someone from the group. She now allows that story to influence her present and future experiences regarding people. It is important for Tamara to remind herself that these people are separate from the ones who hurt her in the past; that there are good men and well-meaning people in the world. Remind yourself of the scriptural principle of sowing and reaping. You will reap in the same likeness of what you sow—a person who wants friends has to be friendly.

Counseling is the next best step for Tamara. She needs a counselor who will challenge her assumptions while role-playing new realities with her.

Mental Filter: Sarah is on her period and having some stomach cramps. She just wants to get through the day. As she walks into the office, the secretary waves to her and brings her a cup of coffee. Later, her boss walks past her office without stopping to chat with her. Sarah feels slighted and grumbles to herself that no one appreciates her and everyone in this organization is rude and obnoxious

Sarah has always seen through the lenses of pain and has not acknowledged the good deed of a colleague earlier in the day. The mental filter is when you single out only the negative events and overlook the positive. It happens in relationships when the husband or wife sees only the negative things that the other person does. Mental filters will activate the faulty pattern of overgeneralization because you start using the "all or nothing" statements. Learn to look for that silver lining in every cloud. It's all about how you choose to let events affect you. In Philippians 4:8, it says, "Fix your thoughts on what is true, and honorable, and right, and pure and lovely and admirable.

Disqualifying the Positive: Summer just bought a new dress. Her friend tells her how flattering the dress looks on her. Summer brushes aside the compliment by saying that the dress is a cheap purchase from Walmart, and she never looks good in anything

I believe that this particular distortion is the most dangerous because it has to do with the mutilation of soul—the ability to cauterize your person until there is a non-person inside of you. Summer feels that she is not enough and does not measure up to expectations. Her story is not that she is having a bad day but that she is inherently damaged. This type of person will refute every positive acknowledgement to satisfy the hungry demon of self-deprecation. You disqualify the positive because you have listened to irrational thoughts of inadequacies and invisibility and cannot entertain thoughts of goodness and well-being. In the case of Summer, what seems like an off-handed comment of humility is a cover for self-damage. People who have this distortion have usually experienced abuse and/or neglect in earlier life. On a continuum of soul mutilation, they could be anywhere from a simple lack of self-awareness to a high level of self-destruction. They will sabotage healthy relationships and gravitate toward dysfunction.

Counseling is the next best step for Summer. She needs a counselor who can do the healing work with her.

Meditation is the cure for shame or soul mutiny. The LORD admonished Joshua to meditate on the Word "both day and night." The process of meditation turns your attention to the reality of who you are and replaces the negative beliefs with scriptures about your beauty and grace; your position in the highest place of authority; your spiritual linage, love and grace; mercy and truth; new creation and the beloved of Christ.

The next time someone compliments you, resist the little voice inside that says that you don't deserve it.

Just say thank you and smile. The more you do this, the easier it will become.

Jumping to Conclusions: Jessica's ex-husband is twenty minutes late to their daughter's soccer game. Jessica begins to get angry because he is irresponsible and inconsiderate. How can he be late for his own daughter's game? However, the ex-husband was late because the roads were closed due to a car-racing event in that city.

In order to maintain a peaceful life, you will need to extend grace to others. Grace is when I get what I do not deserve. Even though your ex-husband does not deserve for you to believe the best because of his past record, you can extend grace to him for the sake of your child. It is a more powerful paradigm. You have the power to withhold *and* to give, but remember whatever you sow will be multiplied back to you in good measures. Be gracious to people, and grace will be multiplied back to you.

Magnification and Minimization: Caroline's husband compliments her on receiving the employee of the month award at work. Caroline's response was that the award was useless to her since her husband didn't attend the ceremony. It is important to note that her husband was not in attendance because their babysitter canceled and he had to stay with the kids.

The rule of thumb is to magnify the good and minimize the bad, not the other way. Caroline minimized her husband's commendation and maximized the faults. There are no perfect relationships, and there can be no perfect situations, so it is important for us to be selective in amplifying the good things in life. Instead of complaining about what your spouse or friend or children haven't done, why not celebrate what they do?

I read a story of a wonderful woman in a particular village who was known for her gracious conversations. She had never said anything negative about anyone in the village, both young and old. Then one day, the most belligerent and wicked man in the village died, and the whole village gathered for his funeral because everyone was sure that for the first time in her life, the gracious woman would not find anything nice to say about the deceased. When it was her turn to eulogize the dead, the woman walked around the casket several times until she turned, faced the crowd, and said, "He sure did have nice teeth."

Celebrate the beauty and goodness in your world. The world may give you lemons, but you can make lemonade. I may not have shoes, but I thank God that I am not without my limbs. Your husband may not be the most romantic guy around, but he may be a great chef in your home. We are not all blessed with the same things, but we all have some things to celebrate.

Our minds can become cesspool of wrong thoughts and ideas. These might be thoughts that were planted in your mind by people you've been in contact with all your life. Since the amygdala, a part of your brain responsible for fear, captures the deepest and strongest of negative emotions to re-experience them, you will find yourself reliving moments of sadness. If your first experience of a relationship was abusive (either you saw our father beat on your mom or someone on the play ground told you how horrible you looked), the amygdala registers your intense reaction to these feelings. Each time you are in the same situation, you will not feel the same unless you experience that primary response. So in relationships, you will seek abuse; in friendships, you will seek hurt and it becomes a self-fulfilling prophecy. You will soon start to notice a pattern in your life and begin to formulate philosophies of austerity, such as: "There is no one to love me." "I am all alone in the world." "There are no good men and all fathers are dead beats." Your life has been driven by experiences of yesteryears that have slowly formed strongholds of hurt, pain, shame, and aloneness. Strongholds are hard to destroy without explosives; you might spend years chipping away at the edges. The stronghold of negative thoughts must be shattered through spiritual weapons that have been shared in this book and sociopsychological tools.

Counseling is highly recommended for this type of paradigm. You do not have to suffer alone. Counselors and therapists are helpers who are trained to assist in your life's journey.

Declarations

- My good now follows me.

- The weapon of doubt cannot keep me from my promised land.

- I am a child of peace and prosperity; I now attract the man of peace and prosperity.

- My thoughts are peaceful, forgiving, and gracious.
- I now attract gold and silver into my life.
- I am beautifully and wonderfully created by my father.
- Spirit dwells within me and is now transforming every imperfection to perfection.
- All negative thoughts that are controlling my life are now silenced; every mutiny holding ground in my mind is now terminated.
- I am not bound by evil thoughts of shame, neglect, inadequacies, and insufficiency. I am surrounded by goodness and mercy. People favor me, and I am blessed all around.
- I am loved spirit, soul, and body.
- Every need in my life is met; every mountain is brought low, and all valleys of need are filled.
- I am restored.
- I am whole and filled with love and peace.
- The grace of God is enough for me. I lack nothing, and there is nothing missing in my life.

Desires Acceptance

Loneliness is separation from Spirit and self. We are whole only when we are spirit-formed and self-aware. Fear of loneliness led to the fall. Adam's fear of being alone led to the eating of the forbidden fruit. He certainly understood that the punishment for disobedience was death. He watched Eve eat of the fruit. We are told that he ate of the fruit of the tree of knowledge of good and evil. What is it about this feeling of physical or emotional aloneness that drove him to condemnation?

Adam fell before he ate the fruit. Jesus explained it to us that whosoever shall look at a person lustfully or even think about it has already committed a sin. Adam's sin was high treason because before he intentionally disobeyed; he had calculated the cost and weighed his options and then chose to be on his wife's side instead of God's side. So why did he do it? Fear of being alone. Adam remembered how excruciatingly painful it was to be desperately lonely pre-Eve days. However, his mandate from his creator was to take authority, keep the land, operate a business, administer animal justice, and protect his wife. The last assignment was his most desperate need, and he did everything to remain with her.

The book of Ecclesiastes tells us that it is good for two people to dwell together, for they have a greater reward. Adam cried out to his God for a helpmate, someone who was comparable to him. He received this beautiful woman and called her Eve because she came out of him. I'm not trying to beat up on Adam here, but the initial problem with him was that he didn't take the time to understand himself before asking for a companion. When the Lord made man, we were told that he made him male and female. When God said, "Let us make man in our own image and likeness," that was exactly what he did. He made Adam complete. Everything Adam ever needed was inside of himself. Because he didn't take the time to recognize and understand himself, it spelled disaster for the human race.

The fear of loneliness is so pervasive in people's lives that it will cause them to marry the wrong person, commit adultery, become alcoholics or shopaholics, become greedy, mistreat people, or become fearful and clingy. Adam's fear of loneliness brought destruction to humanity. Loneliness is separation from self. We are tripartite beings and herein is the problem: the spirit speaks, the soul speaks, and the body speaks. The trio is alive but separate. When the Lord commanded Adam to have dominion, he should have started with himself by aligning spirit, soul, and body. This means that all three parts should have the same purpose. Jesus tells us that a house divided against itself cannot stand. When the three parts or tripartite-being are separated, what we have is dysfunction. The reason we have so many dysfunctional families is because we have men and women, with alienated inward lives, trying to create families. This cannot work. The desires of soul, spirit, and body should be in unison. Any dissonance will result in separation and loneliness.

"Song of the Lonely Woman"

Loneliness is a debt collector,
Going from house to house seeking to gather
   revenue
Fill my cup of emptiness, she cries, because you
   owe me.
I can't be by myself for I am afraid of who
   I'll find.
You owe me a hug. You owe me a kiss!
A touch, a smile or simple hello
You pass me by like darkness at night – not a
nod, nor a sigh; nor a fleeting glance.
My light has become invisible to you.
Loneliness has crawled up in my soul to
   take refuge
You used to love me; you used to hold me; you
used to touch my face with your smile.
We used to make love in the early morning
   light
I wrapped my soul in a blanket and watched
you cradle it gently but the day came when you
flung it on ice
Cold as ice; freezing soul;
I cannot find me in you…there is me!

Merino, 2011

Desires Restoration

The moral of the story of the woman with the issue of blood is that she didn't give up until she was restored. It's not surprising that she is called the woman with the issue. A lot of us have issues that we drag through life. This woman's life was being drained out of her body. Her quality of life had diminished, and she had spent much money trying to recover. Her issue was hidden to the society at large. This disease was feminine and personal. According to Jewish law, she should not be seen in public for fear of her contaminating the men. Her faith increased every time she heard that the master was a healer. Romans 10:17 states that: "Faith comes by hearing and hearing by the word of God." So she kept building her faith by affirming her healing "if only I can touch the hem of His garment, I will be made whole."

She broke the law by venturing out in public for she was considered unclean. But for this hemorrhaging woman, enough was enough. She was tired of her sickness, her poverty, and her public stigma. In order to get healed, she had to do something different. She had to defy customs and self-consciousness. There comes a time when the need is greater than the obstacles. Here was a woman with issues just like you and me. We all have something that is draining the life out of us and until we come to the place of absolute abandonment, there will be no breakthrough. She got herself out of that room, clothed herself, and went in search of the Healer.

I believe that her faith was what brought Jesus to her neck of the woods. Jesus was on his way to heal Jairus's daughter, and there was this woman pressing through the crowd. Jesus knew she was there, because He is all-knowing. He had her answer, but she had to make her way through the crowd to get to him. I sincerely believe that if she had turned back, Jesus would have kept on going to Jairus's house. He knew she needed the healing, but she had to do her part. I also believe that with every step she took, she was getting healed. She was a woman on a mission. She probably said to herself, *There is a reason why I can't turn back now. I have come too far from home and now so close to the miracle. I must touch Jesus, so excuse me learned ones. Excuse me all you spectators. I have a healing to receive.*

She finally got to Jesus, touched the hem of his garment, and received her complete healing. Her goal was to return as unnoticed as she arrived. After all, her sickness was a private battle and had been solved privately. She didn't see any need to testify or to expose herself. The stronghold of self-defeat was still working in her life even though she had just experienced a miracle. This was a woman with low self-esteem because years of house imprisonment had done a number on her. She was the outcast of the society who couldn't and shouldn't be seen in public. What she didn't bargain on was the Jesus who came to restore women back to intimate relationships with him. So Jesus called for her. At that moment when he stopped and asked, "Who touched me?" this woman would have almost died of embarrassment. But Jesus was persistent. He knew that in order for her to get a total healing, she had to give voice to her new condition of health. He called for her again, and this time she took another step of faith to answer him. I believe that it took the same act of faith for her to come out this second time.

Jesus wasn't finished with her yet. He knew that if she wasn't set free from the stronghold of low self esteem; her healing was not complete. So she answered. She came forward and instantly everything became clear. The shy woman whose spirit had died long ago came alive in the presence of the LORD. She testified of her deliverance in the presence of the same people who had disparaged her. She had to overcome the stronghold of her mind. Jesus said to her, "Daughter, you took a risk trusting me, and now you're healed and whole. Live well; live blessed!" We can only live well when we are restored. Jesus called out to her because he wanted to help her in the restoration of her self image. The enemies we wrestle with the most are the hidden schemas and underlying attitudes. If you've been beaten up so long, you might start to believe that you're worthless. If you experienced abuse during childhood, you might start believing that there is no safe haven for you. Schemas are formed by a single experience or a culmination of experiences.

As she testified publicly, she must have experienced a paradigm shift that her life was worth living. The Master reached through the crowds and ministered to one woman and he can do it for you. Keep pressing toward your healing.

> LORD, give me the strength to pursue my miracles. Enable me to take my eyes off all of my problems and focus only on you. I believe that I can search for you in your words, because you will light my lamp. "The LORD my God will enlighten my darkness" (Psalm 18:28). I also know that your words give light; it gives understanding to the simple. I will pursue you, LORD, at this time of need (be specific!). You said in your Word, that if I ask, I will receive; if I seek, I will find; and if I knock, the door will be opened for me, so now I receive the answers to my prayers. Let me see my destination so clearly that I have the strength to push through the crowd of anxiety, fear, people, and my own limited mind.

Desires Intervention

> Now He arose from the synagogue and entered Simon's house. But Simon's wife's mother was sick with a high fever, and they made request of Him concerning her. So He stood over her and rebuked the fever, and it left her. And immediately she arose and served them.
>
> Luke 4: 38–39

We are intercessors in our homes and for our generation. The scriptures posit that we are to rebuild broken bridges of generation past. As soon as Jesus entered Simon's house, the request was made of him to heal the mother-in-law. Who in your family is in need of prayer? Who are you interceding or standing in the gap for in your family? Draw a genogram of your family's challenges, and you will discover the patterns of maladaptive behaviors. This is important if you are to rebuild the broken bridges. There are families who have broken bridges in the spirit realm. Their access to freedom, peace, and grace has been severed by involvememt in the occult, addictions, and generational curses. There are children who are living the consequences of actions that occurred in prior generations.

Whatever the maladaptive behavioral patterns in your family, it is your responsibility to stand as a mediator and bridge builder. Build a bridge to healing, sanity, and peace. You are the miracle that your family has been waiting for. You have the ears of God and that of your people. You are the savior like Esther who is sent to redeem a people. The family is the design of God for redemption. It is in the context of family that we learn to heal, forgive, and restore. There is no other Eden but your home and people. If there is a history of abortion in your family, it is your responsibility to say that it stops in your generation. Bring light to the situation in love, and incrementally your family will embrace life. If there is a history of divorce in your family, you decide that the buck stops with you. Affirm marriage and live it in the presence of your people. Pray for the family and ask the Spirit to intervene in your family system. Families are spiritual systems living out a physical existence, and therefore, can be greatly influenced by the Spirit interventions. Permit the Spirit of life to breathe on the broken state of your family.

Jesus restored the mother-in-law who then began to serve. She was released to do what she loved and that is the beauty of restoration. There are people in your families who are bitter, wounded, sick, and tired. These people live shadow lives because they are prostrated by their limitations. Once we shine the light of Spirit in their direction, they begin to change. Like the metamorphosis of a caterpillar to a butterfly, they will soon begin to fly. You are a catalyst for change in your family. The Savior is in your house. The healer is in your house, and the Spirit lives within you. You are the hands of faith, the mouth of faith, and the legs of faith. It is through you that the Spirit will be released and manifested in your home. The faith healer might never make it to your house, but you live in this space, and the miracle will be transmitted through you.

DECLARATIONS

Spirit of the living God, inhabit my family system.

Breathe peace into my home; restore my people and release them from the grip of iniquity.

I call on the creator to recreate hope and joy in the lives of my children, spouse, brothers, sisters, mother and father.

Healing powers touch spirits, souls, and bodies.

DECLARATION PRAYER

LORD, use me as an instrument of miracles! I am
    willing. Use me!
I receive the wisdom and strength to become the
    voice, hands, and feet of God in this house.
I walk by faith and not by sight.
I choose to believe.
My family is declared well and restored.

DESIRES TO CREATE A GENOGRAM

Family systems theory was introduced by Dr. Murray Bowen and suggests that individuals cannot be understood in isolation from one another but rather as a part of their family, as the family is an emotional unit. Families are systems of interconnected and interdependent individuals, none of whom can be understood in isolation from the system. We are interdependent on each other, thereby affecting or creating behavioral patterns.

According to Bowen, a family is a system in which each member had a role to play and rules to respect. Members of the system are expected to respond to each other in a certain way according to their role, which is determined by relationship agreements. Within the boundaries of the system, patterns develop as certain family members' behavior is caused by and causes other family members' behaviors in predictable ways. Maintaining the same pattern of behaviors within a system may lead to balance in the family system but also to dysfunction. For example, if a husband is depressive and cannot pull himself together, the wife may need to take up more responsibilities to pick up the slack. The change in roles may maintain the stability in the relationship, but it may also push the family toward a different equilibrium. This new equilibrium may lead to dysfunction as the husband's response might be animosity toward the wife for taking his role; the wife feeling overwhelmed and the children might feel a need to choose sides.

A genogram is a visual display of the patterns and medical and mental health history in our families. It is not a traditional family tree but a display of hereditary patterns and psychological variables that impact relationships. It can be used to identify behavioral patterns and tendencies in your family tree. You will use this genogram to gather this type of information that will help you place your maladaptive issues in a broader context of your generational parenting skills, marital relationships, and patterns of problem solving. If "Uncle Steve gets so angry till he punches the wall"; the genogram might help you see that he is not the only male who does that in the family and might also portray the genesis of the problem.

Both a family tree and a genogram of the Johnson family would report that Martin, the son of Eliza and Brian, married Pauline, the daughter of Cory and Gabriella, and together Martin and Pauline have two children, Wally and Florentine.

Using the above example, the genogram could also tell you that Pauline has a conflicting relationship with Gabriella, that Martin is the oldest child with two younger sisters, and that Cory and Gabriella have a distant relationship. The genogram might also show that Martin and Pauline had three miscarriages before Florentine was born and that Martin has troubled relationship with Wally. Genograms show intergenerational patterns of relationships, communication, and other behaviors.

It is important to arm yourself with this information so you can understand that you are part of generational system. Determine how far into the family history you would like to cover—three to four generations is plenty of information. Then you will do the research. Talk to these people with love and grace. This is not a time to be judgmental. The process of gathering information should be approached prayerfully and respectfully. You may look at a family tree to get the names and relationships, but it is important to remember that people are willing to share their stories. Keep information private, and learn to be your brother's keeper. There are various genogram sites on the internet that can help you start the process. A genogram is created with simple symbols representing the gender, with various lines to illustrate family relationships. Symbols might be used to identify some of the information. A key, placed in the bottom right-hand corner of the sheet, should identify the meaning of each symbol. Here is a list of necessary information:

- Names, nicknames, family titles for each person.

- Dates of birth, death, severe illness, marriages, separations, divorces, other rites of passage.

- Physical locations and dates of important moves

- Frequency of contact between members of the extended family or strength and type of relationship. (Double lines may illustrate frequent contact and close relationships. Dashed lines may illustrate distant relationships and infrequent contact. Lines with slashes may illustrate conflict-ridden relationships.)

- Emotional cutoffs. What was the issue or event? When?

- Ethnicity, occupation, socioeconomic level, religious affiliation, and participation., power struggles, alcohol and/or drugs problems.

- Important health and personality characteristics.

People who are adopted and have little or no information about their birth parents can create the genogram on their adopted parents. Genetic-driven health characteristics may play a less important role than other environmental and familial factors.

Here Is a How-to Guideline

1. Decide how many generations to include in your genogram map. List the members of each generation on a piece of paper. Draw lines to divide the people into generational sections.[1]

2. Add these people to your poster board in permanent marker. Start with the oldest generation that you want to include. Indicate a male with a square and a female with a circle. Write the name of each person inside his square or her circle.

3. Show any marriages in the first generation by drawing a line connecting the married couple. Show a divorce by adding a slash through the line that signifies a marriage.

4. Beneath the first generation, list the next generation on your poster board. Connect the first generation to the next generation by drawing lines connecting a couple's children to the line representing the couple's marriage. Do this for each generation as you move down your map. Continue to indicate marriages and divorces in each generation.

5. Add birth and death dates for each person on your map. Include the cause of death if known.

6. Add any information that you want to keep track of, whether it be medical or personal. Be as detailed or as vague as you want about each person on your genogram map.

Once you have identified the dysfunctional pattern in your family, it would be beneficial to talk to a counselor. However, here is a restoration plan that I find powerful. It is faith-based and transcendent:

1. Acknowledge the issue.

2. Acknowledge your source and scriptural promise (The Lord sets free. "He that is set free by the Lord is free indeed; I will not be brought under the bondage of anything…").

3. Acknowledge who you are in the spirit. (I am a child of God; I am set free. You can also add the name of whomever needs freedom).

4. Repudiate the issue in the name of Jesus. (I terminate all spiritual bonds of addiction in the name of Jesus. No addiction is permitted in my family; I sever all agreements with hell, death, and dysfunction; I will not operate under the influence of seducing spirits in my life or my family's life).

5. Pronounce the wellness and peace. (I declare that I am free from all nicotine, gambling, addictions, etc. I am free. I desire only natural nutrients. I am at peace with my spirit, soul, and body. My family is free to enjoy the earth of God).

6. Engender the blood covenant. (I seal this with the blood of Jesus, and it is not permitted to resurrect. Amen).

7. Be thankful. (I am grateful for my freedom and the grace to work out my wellness with patience).

8. Follow up with specific practical action. (Creating an atmosphere that is conducive

to wellness; separating from former addictive influences; seeking therapy to relearn how to live; reading books on how to live the free life, etc.).

9. Never acknowledge the broken system. (You are no longer an addict etc. You are free since the spiritual source has been severed).

10. Declare only what you want. (I am made whole. I have the winning personality. I have the strength to walk away, etc.).

Desires to Communicate

Families repeat patterns across generations as they get trapped in predictable but often unexamined life patterns, which are created in part through their interactions with others. Some of these patterns are communication patterns. Communication within a family context is transactional, which means that our interpretation of what is being said creates our perception of reality. As members of a family interact, they create context for each other and relate to each other within that setting. This creates a pattern that each of them will affect their individual lives.

For example, a mother and sister had a very difficult relationship with each other for many years, although both of them had a great relationship with everyone else in the family. Irene saw her mother as unrelenting and demanding, although the other sibling would characterize her as serious and concerned. Mom saw Irene as lackadaisical and uncommitted, although no one else saw her that way. Whenever they tried to talk to each other, each responded to the person she created, and it was a continual battle.

We respond to our perception of others and not necessarily what they are saying. It is therefore necessary to understand that what you are feeling might not be the whole truth in this moment. Doubt your doubts and starve your negative thoughts of self and others. Communication with family is an integral part of our existence since relationships are erected on this foundation.

What Is the Transcendent Communication Process?

- For communication to happen there must be a sender (who conveys a message) and a receiver (to whom the message is sent).

- In successful communication, the sender is clear and accurately conveys the message she is trying to send. Also, the receiver clearly understands the message.

- Miscommunication occurs if the sender does not send a clear message and/or the receiver does not understand the message sent by the sender.

- Sandwich the bad within the good. Always start with good and end with the solutions.

Never leave anyone (including your loved ones) hopeless.

- The purpose of communication is to bring us into agreement. There is power in connection, and when there is miscommunication there is disunity and strife.

Many things can get in the way of good communication. For example:

1. When we assume we know what others are thinking or that they should know what we are thinking.

2. When we focus on what we want to say while others are talking, instead of listening to them.

3. When we bring up other problems and issues unrelated to the topic at hand.

4. When we assume we know what is right for others and try to convince them of this.

All of these things either keep us from sending a clear message or keep us from receiving the message the other person is trying to send.

Communication between the Sexes

We must understand the communication patterns of the sexes, because males and females communicate differently. The man's mind is compartmentalized and organized like a chest of drawers while the woman's mind is interconnected. Imagine a situation where James and Jessica are middle-level managers at work; they have been given a project that is due at the end of the week. James and Jessica suffered some personal loss during that same week; however, they will respond differently because of the way they process information. James gets to work about the same time as Jessica, and he is relieved to immerse himself in this project. He does not think about the family or the loss suffered when he is at work since the only 'drawer' pulled is the work drawer. Jessica, on the other hand, is working as hard, but she cannot help but think about the impact of the loss on her children and spouse and how it would affect her aging parents. She also has to think about how this will impact her career. She even wonders if it might be wise to speak with the pastor this afternoon. Jessica's loss is related to all the other things and people in her life. James was able to compartmentalize his feelings regarding his personal problem so he can focus at work whereas Jessica works while ruminating on the ramifications of all her loss.

How does this impact communication? Imagine an argument between you and your spouse about taking out the trash. Once you initiate the conversation about trash, your husband's or boyfriend's trash 'drawer' is pulled open, and he is ready to speak about trash; however, you only start with the trash as a starting point. However, by the time the conversation is over, you have connected the fact that he didn't take the trash out to the way he loves you, his mother's irreverent behavior towards you, his friends attitude, and that time during vacation five years ago when he forgot to open the car door for you. The poor guy is speechless as he stares at you wondering what all these have to do with trash. So you see, the woman's interconnected mind does not allow for fair competition when it comes to communicating with the opposite sex. The woman should learn to focus on the topic of discussion because not everything is connected. Forgetting to take out the trash might be just that, not a conspiracy to sabotage your relationship.

Active listening is a way of listening to others that lets them know you are working to understand the message they are sending. It is about honoring the spirit of the person speaking to you. When we pay attention to the other person, we are directly paying homage to the greater good in them. When this happens, the higher self in them will rise to the occasion and respond in kind. Our problem in communication is that we respond from our lowest self, which is selfish, hurtful, vindictive and manipulative, and we wonder why we don't get rewarded in kindness. The ultimate communication principle is to speak to the highest self in the other person, and wake up the good, kind, and loving. Communicating well takes practice and effort. It is not something that comes naturally for most of us. However, your conversations and relational transactions will change when you focus on listening to the other person, rather than thinking of your next response.

There are four types of communication patterns that form the basis of how we express ourselves. Aggressive communication is a type of communication pattern which involves manipulation. We may attempt to make people do what we want by inducing guilt (hurt) or by using intimidation and control tactics (anger). Covert or overt, we simply want our needs met—and right now! Although there are a few arenas where aggressive behavior is called for (i.e., sports or war), it will never work in a relationship. The aggressive communicator is only interested in her own opinions which she thinks are consistently right. Aggressive communication is born of low self-esteem (often caused by past physical and/or emotional abuse), unhealed emotional wounds, and feelings of powerlessness. She will believe or say phrases like, "I am always right and always have the correct answer," "I can intimidate you," and "I'll get my way no matter what."

Passive communication is based on compliance and hopes to avoid confrontation at all costs. In this mode we don't talk much, we question even less, and actually do very little. We just don't want to rock the boat. Passives have learned that it is safer not to react and better to disappear than to stand up and be noticed. Passive communication is usually born of low self-esteem. These individuals believe: "I'm not worth taking care of." As a result, passive individuals do not respond overtly to hurtful or anger-inducing situations. Instead, they allow grievances and annoyances to mount, usually unaware of the buildup. But once they have reached their high tolerance threshold for unacceptable behavior, they are prone to explosive outbursts, which are usually out of proportion to the triggering incident. After the outburst, however, they feel shame, guilt, and confusion, so they return to being passive. She will believe or say phrases like, "I'm unable to stand up for my rights" and "People never consider my feelings."

A combination of styles, passive-aggressive avoids direct confrontation (passive), but attempts to get even through manipulation (aggressive). If you've ever thought about making that certain someone who needs to be "taught a thing or two" suffer (even just a teeny bit), you've stepped pretty close to (if not on into) the devious and sneaky world of the passive-aggressive. This woman believes that there is a lack of power in the relationship and will therefore destabilize the status quo while appearing accommodating. Women who develop a pattern of passive-aggressive communication usually feel powerless, stuck, and resentful. Instead, they express their anger by subtly undermining the object (real or imagined) of their resentments. They smile at you while setting booby traps all around you. She will say or believe that, "I will appear cooperative, but I'm not."

Assertive communication is the most effective and healthiest form of communication. It's how we naturally express ourselves when our self-esteem is intact, giving us the confidence to communicate without games and manipulation. When we are being assertive, we work hard to create mutually satisfying solutions. We communicate our needs clearly and forthrightly. We care about the relationship and strive for a win/win situation. We know our limits and refuse to be pushed beyond them just because someone else wants or needs something from us. Surprisingly, assertive is the style most people use least. Assertive communication is born of high self-esteem. These individuals value themselves, their time, and their emotional, spiritual, and physical needs, and are strong advocates of self while being very respectful of the rights of others. The assertive communicator will believe or say phrases like, "I respect your right to be have your own opinion," "I will not be your judge," and "I can't control others, but I can control myself." Assertive communication will work well with anyone, especially your spouse. Men do not want to be bossed around like the aggressive communicator does, and they want to be right. The assertive communicator can acknowledge "You are right," while making sure that she is heard.

It takes more than words to create satisfying, strong relationships. Nonverbal communication has a huge impact on the quality of your personal and professional relationships. What you communicate through your body language and nonverbal signals affects how others see you, how well they like and respect you, and whether or not they trust you. Nonverbal communication is a rapidly flowing back-and-forth process. Successful nonverbal communication depends on your ability to manage stress, recognize your own emotions, and understand the signals you're sending and receiving. This requires your full concentration and attention. If you are planning what you're going to say next, daydreaming, or thinking about something else, you are almost certain to miss nonverbal cues and other subtleties in the conversation. You need to stay focused on the moment-to-moment experience in order to fully understand what's going on. If you're feeling overwhelmed by stress, it's best to take a time out. Take a moment to calm down before you jump back into the conversation. Once you've regained your emotional equilibrium, you'll be better equipped to deal with the situation in a positive way.

Finally, the basic ingredient for effective communication is love. Love always seeks the good of the other person. Love is patient and kind. This also means that love will not use hurried speech and will be patient enough to allow for a response and clarity. Love comes from within, and it manifests itself in your smile, voice, and posture. A loving person is one who looks at her world with kindness, a virtue that is extended to all whom she encounters. A woman who loves will find it easy to forgive and extend grace; however, one who is unkind or unloving to herself will find it extremely frustrating trying to be nice to people. You cannot give what you lack. Cultivate a loving attitude by forgiving yourself, and it will extend to others around you.

Desires Worship

The woman referred to as the town harlot brought a gift to Jesus in the middle of the day. This woman was rejected, abused, and condemned, but she reached out to Jesus though the mess in worship. This woman realized that the only hope for her deliverance was with the Lord. She did not focus her attention on the mitigating circumstances and accusers in her life. The disciples had gotten too familiar with Jesus and did not draw from the anointing or appreciate the person in their presence. The host and his friends reveled in the knowledge of the scriptures and were intoxicated with their own successes. It was customary to wash the visitors' feet as they had traveled dusty roads, but as we see, this was not offered to Jesus.

This woman knew that she was a failure on several levels, but she still reached into the archives of her life and found a valuable piece. She kept her eyes focused on the Master, and his loving eyes drew her closer. She broke the alabaster box and worshiped him. She gave him all that she had, and in return, she was memorialized and accepted by the Lord. Some bring the alabaster box, but they only offer droplets to the Lord. There are times when you need to give all that you have in order to transcend. You will receive much more than you gave because you will now make contact with your solution.

You are a woman by design, and the purpose for your life is to transcend from the miry clay of the suffering and abuse. This woman had prostituted herself and was drained of glory and beauty. She suffered in the hands of molesters, and her own lack of self-identity destroyed her image. She probably heard of Jesus restoring sight to the blind and healing the sick; maybe even raising the dead. But she had not heard of him healing the mind. How would he reach down into her psyche to perform a miracle of grace? She wasn't sure, but she knew that he was her saving grace. If this man could not help then there was no longer hope for her. She received much more than she gave. Some of you are holding on to your last valuable possession or might even think that you do not have anything of value. It is time to break the best that you have for the master.

A significant gift allows you to sow into your destiny. Whatever you give yourself to, will give back to you in good measures, pressed down and shaken together. Picasso gave himself to art, and it is still giving back to him today. Mandela gave himself for freedom, and it gave him a free nation. Jesus poured himself as an offering for humanity, and his church is now counted in billions. Give significantly, and you will see the tides move favorably towards you. The tendency is to hoard during austerity, but the principle of the kingdom is the way out is through gifting.

Desires Forgiveness

Worship is intimacy, and we expose ourselves in the process. We were made to worship the LORD. We can do this by how reverent we live our lives. Some live their lives as if it is not valuable or significant. Some live a selfish existence of greed and lawlessness. Their life song is melancholic and distressed. It is the height of arrogance to live a life devoid of grace and forgiveness. If your life reflects a lack of gratitude, then you have thumbed your nose at your Maker and decided that you are alone. A life of worship is lived in awe and gratitude. Your career can reflect your life song. The way your raise your family and how you deal with the affairs of your life. Worship is not simply singing a song but allowing the spirit of gratitude to be your life's song. You are a worshipper when you are spirit-formed and spirit-led.

If we add the story of the woman caught in act of adultery who was dragged to Jesus and that of the town harlot, we will find that they were both identified by their sins. Both were women stigmatized by society. They were harlots and adulterers. The adulterer was dragged to Jesus with hardly any clothes to maintain her dignity while the town harlot was harassed for her audacity. These women lived on the fringes of society. They were outcasts. We have to understand that their sins were publicly identified and judged. The first century Jewish women had no rights. A woman caught in the act of adultery was dragged to Jesus while the man was probably lounging in his house. Women were shamed and killed for sexual sins while their partners looked the other way. The twenty-first century hypocrites are too civilized to cast physical stones, but we will condemn the sinners to hell. We will scream at the woman who had an abortion or left her "Christian" abusive spouse as if there is no forgiveness for her. A minister can cheat on his wife and be forgiven while the woman is left to fend for herself. Grace is to be extended to every child of God. The scripture says that where sin abounds, grace did much more abound. However, this same grace should be applicable to the women in our churches.

I am yet to find hierarchies of sin in the New Testament. A sinner is like fish in the water: it can't help but swim. We all simply have different bodies of water we swim in. Some fish are in a tiny aquarium while others make their homes in the Atlantic Ocean. The one thing they have in common is their fluid environment and their nature. A fish cannot help but swim and neither can a sinner help but commit sin. Paul agonized over this in the book of Romans. The sinner (one whose life hasn't been touched by the Holy Spirit) cannot help him or herself. Romans 3:23 states that, "Since we've compiled this long and sorry record as sinners (both us and them) and proved that we are utterly incapable of living the glorious lives God wills for us…" (The Message).

Am I advocating or excusing sins? No! Romans 6:12 asks the same question, "So what do we do? Keep on sinning so God can keep on forgiving? I should hope not! If we've left the country where sin is sovereign, how can we still live in our old house there?" A sinner cannot help but commit sin. The Apostle Paul gave a list of sins in Romans 1 including but not limited to homosexuality, adultery, greed, envy, jealousy, murder, strife, deceit, treachery, ill will, cruel ways, backbiters, and gossipers. I don't hear the religious pundits crying out against the gossip or deceit that's actually going on in the church. The need of human beings to set up power structures and categories of sins is a reflection of a powerless church who demonstrates religiosity, having a form of holiness but denying the power thereof (2 Timothy 3:5). This is still the dispensation of grace. No matter how much we want to rain fire and brimstone upon others, the message of the cross is still grace and mercy. It is the goodness of the LORD that leads us to repentance. Jesus challenged the religious zealots of his day, "Let him who has no sin cast the first stone" (John 8:7). Should women keep killing their babies? No! Can divorcees find forgiveness in Christ Jesus? Yes! Our ministry is that of reconciliation.

There are women sitting in our churches that have had abortions and can't find a place of forgiveness. How long will Rachel cry for her children? The mercy of God is potent enough to forgive and cleanse us from all righteousness. I am talking to women out there who have those hidden sins. You've committed adultery. You've had an abortion or two. You've tried alternative lifestyles. There is no sin too powerful that cannot be cleansed by the blood of Jesus. Everyone needs a Savior, and you can find solace in him. He who the LORD sets free is free indeed.

Until we find the emptiness in our souls, we cannot obtain the fullness of his mercy. Forgiveness is freely given to those who surrender. This is why we cry out for mercy and not justice. Who can stand before the judgment of a great God? It was mercy that drew the harlot to the feet of Jesus that day. With angry eyes watching, this woman make a fool of herself by crying and kissing his feet. With every drop of tears and whispering kiss, she was crying for acceptance. "I know they condemn me Lord, but I've heard that you are the lover of lost souls." Do you accept me Lord? She was begging not to be rejected and alienated. There was no better place to start a new life but at the feet of Jesus. Without a spoken word, she offered Him all of her being, knowing that she would not be turned away. In that moment she was accepted into the loving arms of the Savior. In a single moment she went from a sinner to the beloved. Another daughter of Abraham returned to her position of honor. The Lord defended her actions of love and surrender, affirming the principle of engagement—abandoned love and worship flows freely from the heart of one who is forgiven much.

> Lord, restore me to my position of honor. Teach me how to worship you selflessly. I now count my blessings… indeed goodness and mercy will encircle me all of my days. Thank you for accepting and restoring me by your grace. Continue to be my mighty defense against all hostilities. Protect me from becoming marginalized or a stereotype. Help me maintain my integrity as a woman of purpose that I may demonstrate your hope for humanity.

Desires a Definite Word

The woman at the well needed a definite word from Jesus. She was a five-time divorcee who was "shacking up" with another man. Imagine this woman in the twenty-first century church! Husbands would warn their wives to keep away from her. She would hear enough condemnation to extinguish any glimmer of hope. But Jesus broke with tradition to answer the deepest cry of a broken woman. He walked through her pain to touch the hidden places of her heart with healing and powerful words of restoration. The spoken word transformed this "messed up" woman into an evangelist. A word from God will quiet the storms of self-destruction, loneliness, and disillusionment and transform us into women of passion and purpose.

Women are powerful tools in the Master's hands. The pages of history are laced with women who dared to make a difference. Our struggles, hopes, and dreams create a beautiful mantle of passionate pursuit, a group of powerful women ready to change their world. Instead of emphasizing our separateness and independence, it seems that our strength lies in being knitted together in kingdom pursuit.

Words are powerful because they are carriers of hope and destiny. An encounter with life changing words can transform lives. It should certainly light a fire on the inside. Hopefully, you will see, think, and act differently. Faith filled words allow you to see with eternal eyes. It envisions what others cannot fathom. It visualizes you as a powerful woman, even in the midst of a turbulent dynamic. Faced with the appearance of wayward, disobedient, and unruly situations, you keep your calm assurance that "all is well and all manner of things will be well." Your confidence is not based on external experiences that are temporary rather focus on intrinsic persuasions which have enough power to change circumstances.

So when your family struggles to meet the basic necessities of life or faces the loss of a child, sickness, or loneliness, you need a word of affirmation and purpose that will uphold truth in your heart. Transformation happens from the inside out. We must see the truth within ourselves before it can be projected out like a movie onto screens of our lives. We are to command the revelation of truth to our circumstance. What else but faith could comprehend the fact that you will become a successful writer, even though you've never received any training? Who can fathom your being a powerful mother with spiritual children, when your mother was abusive or absent? Words of faith helps you venture out of your prison of limitation and dream bigger than your circumstances.

GRATITUDE IN THE DRY PLACES

Gratitude is the attitude of a heart that is dependent on grace. It is the response of the believer who is committed to the principle of dependence. We live in a world of murmuring and complaining. It is a technologically advanced generation who seek tomorrow instead of living today. There is a malaise of indifference and ingratitude that has permeated the lives of the twenty-first-century community who refuse to give glory to God or acknowledge the workings on the spirit in their lives. We were created to give God pleasure. The book of Revelations states: "…we were created for his pleasure" (Revelation 4:11).

We give him pleasure when he sees us enjoying the life that he gave us instead of putting it on hold for a tomorrow we have not yet seen. We do not radiate joy when we live lives of ingratitude and desperation. Depression and stress has drained the twenty-first-century woman of her joy and gratitude. Most women are overworked and struggle with the multiplicity of their roles in society. It is difficult to have a heart of gratitude when so much is expected of us. The story of the Hebrew children in captivity demonstrates this struggle between gratitude and personal limitations. The Hebrew children were captured by the Babylonians who had heard stories of their songs of praise. When the captors asked them to sing their songs in the foreign land, the Hebrews could not muster a verse. Instead, they hung their heads and harps down, singing the dearth songs of lost dreams and homes. Their story was one of longing and desperation for a better place and a better land. We too are always wishing for a better life and perceive our present lives as inadequate. We are constantly in disequilibrium and the thought of leaning into our present circumstances is uncomfortable.

The captive Israelites were told to master their strange places.

This is the text of the letter that the prophet Jeremiah sent from Jerusalem to the surviving elders among the exiles and to the priests, the prophets, and all the other people Nebuchadnezzar had carried into exile from Jerusalem to Babylon. It said,

"This is what the LORD Almighty, the God of Israel, says to all those I carried into exile from Jerusalem to Babylon: "Build houses and settle down; plant gardens and eat what they produce. Marry and have sons and daughters; find wives for your sons and give your daughters in marriage, so that they too may have sons and daughters. Increase in number there; do not decrease. Also, seek the peace and prosperity of the city to which I have carried you into exile."

There is a time and season for every divine plan in your life, and when you pray for rain in the rain season, it will pour on you. When we pray for rain in the dry seasons, we can get drops here and there, and even a shower here and there, but it will never be an outpouring season, because there is an order in the world. The children of Israel had their focus on getting the perfect season, and they lost sight of LORD of all seasons. He reminded the Israelites that this is their moment of gratitude. Plant, marry, procreate, harvest, and pray today because the here and now is also significant. Do not put today on hold for the promise of tomorrow. Living is for today. Regardless of how hectic or unpleasant the present situation, we can still find a place of gratitude.

Ruth, the foreign woman and one of only two women to have a book named after her in the Bible, understood the principle of living in the here and now. She had a future as the great-grandmother of King David, but she still had to endure the travel from Moab to Bethlehem attached to a bitter mother-in-law, Naomi. She harvested unwanted grains in the field and followed the instructions of her mentor. The result is a wonderful story of grace and mercy. She is listed in the pages of scripture in the genealogy of the LORD Jesus Christ.

David was anointed king of Israel as a young man of about twenty years, but he did not actually become the king of all of Israel until he was thirty-seven years old. He spent seventeen years or more ministering to the King Saul, befriending the young man Jonathan, fleeing for his life, and making warriors of the destitute who came to him at the cave Adullam (his hiding place).

Jacob could be described as an indentured servant to his uncle and father-in-law because he had to work fourteen years for two wives when he only requested and wanted one. After this arrangement was over, Laban, his father-in-law, got him to stay six more years. During this period, his wages were changed ten times, and there was competition and jealousy from his brother-in-laws. There was competition between the two wives and their maidservants for Jacob's affection. By the time the manipulations, triangulations, and emotional rollercoasters were complete, there were twelve children born who later became the tribes of Israel. A people who are so ingrained in the plans of eternity that they have the pearly gates names after them, "And she had a great and high wall with twelve gates and twelve angels at the gates and names written on them, which are the names of the twelve tribes of the children of Israel."

During this time, Jacob never stopped living his life and serving his God, even though there was a promise of a better tomorrow. Little did he know that he was creating his miracle one mess at a time; one child at a time; one mistake at a time. The time invested with the wicked Laban pales at the attainment of a celestial place in glory. If he had hung his head in gloom, waiting for a better tomorrow, his story would be reminiscent of most of humanity. He came; he lived and died! No legacy; no tributes; no glory.

You can never be stuck if you choose to live a grateful life in the dry places. Faith is an action verb that permits us to walk while we wait. Your life today might not be your promised dream, but it is your life, and the choice to be grateful is more powerful than sorrow. You may not like your situation today, but your God is ever present, and that is a reason to be thankful.

You are creating your miracle now. The gratitude should arise in your hearts because miracles happen in contradictions. You can't have a testimony without a test. There is no other human being that is well equipped to live the life you were destined to live. The twists and the turns on the road will be used by your God to deliver your divine purpose. You are creating your destiny, one choice at a time. If you knew better, you would do better, but you are doing the best you can with the light you have. Stop beating yourself up. You will be liberated if you surrender the need for control. You have the opportunity to turn your rented apartment into a place of joy while you are waiting for the promise of house ownership. You could volunteer in the children's ministry while you are waiting for the promise of your own child. Make the best of the situation without complaining; refuse to mope; refuse to waste any more time pining away for Jerusalem when the LORD declares that you can thrive in Babylon. If we truly serve the God of all the earth, then we will honor him with our lives of gratitude.

If indeed our LORD is sovereign, then today is your perfect time. Now is your day of salvation. Your miracle is in the house today. There is no deliverer coming because you are God's deliverer for your family. You are the source of light. You are the balm and grace. You are his hands extended and grace poured. You are not a mistake, and your life is not a wave of accidents. All things will work in your favor if you make your place in the Spirit. The Apostle Paul encourages us to forget those things that happened yesterday and keep our focus on today. Do not waste another moment pining away for an unrequited love, a lost job, or position. All energies must be mustered into the life that we live today. Give thanks because you are in the right place at the right time.

Jesus the Messiah was aware of his future destination, sitting at the right hand of Majesty, yet he walked the dusty roads of Jerusalem, broke bread with the Twelve, blessed the little children, attended weddings, dined with sinners, cried with friends, wept over homeland, made breakfast for his friends, taught the word, healed the sick, prayed, meditated, and died on a cross—the worst punishment for a thief. Jesus understood the principle of moments. He lived the life of one who had divinity in Him. He taught us to live a life without limits in a world that tries to contain us. He encouraged Peter to get out of his boat of uncertainty, and in a single moment, another man walked on water. We are all God's children, but he is not pleased with everyone because some choose to stay in the boat.

Declarations

- I am in God's plan.
- I am a child of destiny.

Soul Desires

- My life is in perfect harmony with the spirit.
- I can believe for the future, but I can only live in today.
- I choose to be grateful.

DESIRES TO RAISE GOOD CHILDREN

> Children are a gift from the LORD
> They are a reward from him
> Children born to a young man
> Are like arrows in a warrior's hands
> How joyful is the man whose quiver is full
>   of them!
> He will not be put to shame when he confronts
>   his accusers at the gate.
>
> Psalm 127: 3 –5, NLT

Children are like arrows in the hands of a warrior. A warrior is a person habitually engaged in war and/or skilled in the waging of war. This person is a champion, who has perfected the act of winning. In order for women to understand this concept of arrows and children, they must first be acquainted with winning. The truth is, you cannot train someone to win if you have no winning schema or have not experienced victory. The Bible calls you a great warrior who should have experience with success.

Arrows were constructed to penetrate the enemy's shields and were only carried and used by great warriors. Arrows are projectile weapons, which mean that they are offensive, not protective. The arrows had heads made of flint, which were replaced by bronze heads in the second millennium. However, the arrowheads could vary considerably, and some were even blunt (probably used more for hunting small game). Our children are weapons in our hands to pierce all forms of obstacles on planet Earth.

As co-creators with the Father, we not only have the responsibility of birthing these children, we also have the duty of pointing them toward their destiny. Through spending time with the Father and through experiences with our children, we will understand what their purpose is in the world. Children come into this world with gifts and talents, and it our duty to help them discover and develop them. It is our duty to aim the arrow (the child) toward the target (gifts, talents, skills) in order for them to actualize their purpose on earth. Once you find out that one child is musically or artistically talented, you would help prepare by providing the right environment to nurture the gift.

The behavioral theorist Watson said, "Give me a dozen healthy infants, well-formed, and my own specified world to bring them up in and I'll guarantee to take any one at random and train him to become any type of specialist I might select—doctor, lawyer, artist, merchant-chief and, yes, even beggar-man and thief, regardless of his talents, penchants, tendencies, abilities, vocations, and race of his ancestors." This, in essence, supports the premise of this scripture. If you prepare create the proper environment, the children have a better chance of succeeding, and the adverse environment could severely limit the child. An arrow is useless if it is not utilized. Shooting the arrow in parenting simply means that you prepare your children for success in the world. A significant reason for apathy and laziness is because children are unchallenged and uninvolved. Children need their talents developed and minds trained for excellence in a competitive and challenging world. Jochebed is an example of a woman who was a master archer. Who wouldn't want to trade places with this powerful lady? She was the mother of Miriam, Aaron, and Moses. Miriam later became a prophetess; Aaron the first high priest of Israel whose rod remained in the ark of covenant; and Moses, the greatest leader and intercessor in history. Moses would have remained in anonymity if this woman had not shot the arrow. Her placement of Moses in a basket was not an act of abandonment; it was an act of absolute dependence on God. Every mother will have those moments when the odds are against your children and all you can do is knock on heaven's door.

We must have complete confidence in a God, who is absolutely loving and powerful to direct those arrows. Our part is to shoot the arrows, and the Father's part is to make the weather conducive. Jochebed's part was to place baby Moses in a basket and release him into his destiny. I am not sure how much Jochebed knew that this child was destined for greatness. She might not have known that he would end up in Pharaoh's house or that he would lead his people out of bondage. She had no knowledge that he would declare the glory of God to a people who had been devoid of revelation for four hundred years. If she had seen all this, her actions would have made sense to us. However, she did the best thing for Moses in that particular time, and it had to suffice. Sometimes you might not see the entire picture, but you can be the best parent at this very moment. Tomorrow comes in bits of experience so we must maximize each moments with our children. Some parents spent their time becoming friends with their children instead of training them. This will always never end favorably for the child.

There are three types of parenting skills that I would like to share with you. The authoritarian parent is the type you may have grown up with, especially if you can complete this statement, "Children are to seen and not…" This type of parent believes that they have final input in decisions, and children are to follow rules without questioning. The child has little or no input into the policies instituted to guide his or her life, and failure to follow rules result in punishment. Psychologists have called this the most unproductive, destructive, and closed parenting style because it breeds rebellion and anger. I beg to differ as this method seemed to have produced children who have influenced and impacted the trajectory of nations. Everything must be done in moderation.

The authoritative parent, on the other hand, establishes rules and guidelines for the child. However, this parent is more democratic and open to input from the child. Rules can be modified if the child has justifiable reasons to do so. The authoritative parent is more willing to forgive and amend if the child breaks a rule. Parenting is a dualism, not a monopoly.

The permissive parenting style is becoming more pervasive in our society because parents have become maids and friends to children. This generation of parents makes no demand on their children and will sometimes do for them what should be done by them. Visit any elementary school before or after school is out, and you will find parents shuffling backpacks and carrying musical instruments for their kids while they skip to school or home unencumbered. Parents do laundry and pack lunch for high school students. How will your child become industrious when they are fed answers and sheltered from burdens of development?

The most effective type of parenting, in my opinion, is one where parents function in the role of life facilitator and guide. A parent should bless their child with hope and good will while allowing them to stumble and sometimes fall. We must see our children through the eyes of faith. We must provide guidance, while believing that the one who gave them life will guide them to success. The world still seeks major discoveries. There are planets and galaxies waiting to be discovered. There are books that must be penned. There are encounters with God that must be experienced. There are master planners who must come from this community of women.

Children find themselves blowing in the wind of despair, because they can't seem to find a path to belong.

These children become adults who are desperate for a purpose. Children become purposeful when parents begin to parent. We are responsible for their destinies, and I believe that this is one of the major undertakings of all mothers. If we point the child in the direction of purpose, they will have an anchor to weather the storms of life. Parenting is not for the light hearted. Imagine how Jochebed must have felt placing her son in that lonely basket. We must always seek to protect, train, and love the children. Protecting and loving our children is easy; it is the training aspect that stretches us. Training is molding the child and helping him or her conform to the image of destiny within. We should set these three parental mandates as default buttons: protect, train, and love.

We understand that Mary, the mother of Jesus, nurtured the promise while risking societal shame and injustice. She carried a pregnancy of promise the same way you and I carry promises. We nurture and care for them in our stomachs and then sometimes lose sight of the promise. Every child is a promise. Every child is a possibility. They are born with purpose, and it is our duty to create favorable environments.

Our individual disadvantages should not become stumbling stones for the children we birth into this world. The struggling mother of E.V. Hill, the now deceased fiery Baptist preacher, sensed the potential inherent in the child. Against all odds, she pointed him in the direction of education when educating black children was not the norm. She needed him in the fields for sheer survival, but this mother was a champion. She understood that she had to point him in the direction of a school, and she did. He graduated top in his high school class (was the only one in his class) and was later accepted into the A&M University. She bought him a bus ticket to Prairie View with all the money she had and gave him a lunch sack. She told him before getting into that bus, "I will be praying for you." Edward trusted his mother's prayers because he had seen the result numerous times. There he stood in the registration line with $1.83 in his pocket, not knowing how he would pay for his tuition. He was almost to the cashier's counter when someone called his name, informing him that he had been awarded a full four-year scholarship (Los Angeles Times, Feb. 25, 2003).

E.V. Hill later became the senior pastor of the Mount Zion Missionary Baptist Church in the Watts section of Los Angeles where he served for over forty years. Hailed by *Time* magazine as "one of the most outstanding preachers in the United States," he received several doctoral degrees and changed his world in the process. What if Mother Hill had succumbed to the lowest common denominator of ease? We sometimes take the easy road because it doesn't require anything from us. It would have been easy for him to withdraw from secondary school like most black boys of his generation. Who knows what would have happened to Hill. He could still have arrived at his destination with much agony and pain. Instead, the champion warrior thrust him out into his path and trusted the Greater One to direct his paths.

What is your story? What is your legacy? Are you thrusting the arrows of success or simply shooting the daggers of desolation?

Desires Abundance

> Now to Him who by ... the power at work within us is able to do superabundantly far over and above all that we dare ask or think beyond our highest prayers, desires, thoughts, hopes or dreams
>
> Ephesians 3:20, AMP

The desire of the Great Mind of this universe is for his children to exceed expectations; however, because some have experienced lack in life, we have no model for abundance. Most of the country lives paycheck to paycheck—we pay monthly bills with absolutely no savings or assets. Women of faith should reprogram their minds for prosperity. The scripture promises us superabundance according to the power at work within us. We can therefore surmise that the clearer our revelation of God and his purpose, the brighter our light will shine in this world. I have always been challenged by Jesus's admonishment to let your light shine because a city set on a hill cannot be hidden. As a woman of destiny, you are able to radiate the majesty of the kingdom. As a representative of the kingdom, your orders and resources must come from above. "Thy will be done on earth as it is in heaven." This phrase is a call to abundance. If heaven is home to superabundance then our prayer is to reflect heaven's feast on earth.

The question that concerns us is: whose light are we reflecting? If we understand that all things are possible to those who believe then we can appreciate that we have the ability to manifest light around us. Self-help programs have infiltrated our society, leaving us with methodologies without the power. It is insufficient to understand the process of change without the intrinsic power to complete the process. The reason some still live in mediocrity is related to the connection between thoughts and actions. You are not wealth deficient; you are simply thought deficient. You are one thought away from your next success. You will always manifest your deepest thoughts because your actions are extension of thoughts. Why is it that you've prayed for God to bless your family financially and you've even tithed and given offerings to the church and needy, and yet you've remained in the same place of lack for years? You give to support ministries but get nothing in return. What is going on? You believe in divine provision but seem to be a missing element. What happened to the *doing* part? God will bless the works of your hands! We need to give God something to bless. We need to provide a channel for the abundant blessings. We are creative beings. The divine inspiration orchestrated in the beginning of time mandates self-expression. It is the divine purpose for us to meet needs. There cannot be lack if you are meeting needs in the world. This is why we are constantly seeking, knocking, and asking. We must seek in to order to find, ask to receive, and knock for the door to open. A body at rest will remain stagnant until a force is exerted against it; we were born to triumph. There is enough power us is enough to manifest destiny. Everything needed for this journey has been provided. Our duty is to ask for inspiration and enlightenment. Our responsibility is to make a connection with our hearts. Laziness is the number-one reason people stay in the place of lack. We are in the same place of need because of our inability to dig a little deeper, seeking creative thoughts.

Our lives should be undeniable as we reflect the glory within. Our purpose is to win the prize in every area of our lives. We are women of light, and our lights should shine brightly for the nations. The creator manifested destiny when he brought Eve to the place of plenty, a woman so self-contained that she supplied the needs of her husband and her universe. The Proverbs 31 woman was creative and industrious, a producer who never lacked for anything.

Desires Self-Esteem

Your mind is the center of intelligence and control room of life. Once the conscious mind has arranged the muscles, nerves, cells, tissues, and their coordination necessary to perform its task, it relegates their repetition to the subconscious part of the mind. It is only when we are confronted with problems or situations outside of ordinary experience that the conscious mind starts to work, because a new theme is involved. Most of our lives are relegated to subconscious mind operation. It is important to train our minds because when it shifts into the unconscious mode, it takes significant effort to retrain. For example, if you've failed math all your life, your mind will make a note of the fact that you react negatively to the subject, and it will send you that message as soon as you make contact with mathematical concepts. The actions of the mind become subconscious, but this is not a permanent state. You can retrain your mind. Remember, you have control over what goes in and out of your mind. This is why I suggest that you don't hang around with people who put you down because once your mind feeds on that garbage, it registers and spews it back to you.

You can retrain your mind by surrounding yourself with positive influences. If you've heard how ugly or unworthy you are growing up, the only way you can change that is by saturating yourself with powerful and positive words. It's not foolish to stand in front of the mirror and say how beautiful, smart, and worthy you are. Surround yourself with people that will encourage you and assist you on your road to excellence.

What is Self-Esteem?

Self-esteem is "how much a person likes, accepts, and respects himself overall as a person." Researchers have divided the definition into three parts:

- Internal Locus of Control (LOC):

    This factor is how you define the things that happen to you. Are they a series of accidents, or are they your path to success? LOC is your ability to take your life by the reins and get to the finish line. Using your power and control responsibly will build internal locus of control.

- Sense of belonging and acceptance:

    This factor reflects how much you feel wanted and a part of your group (family, community, etc.), and how much you like and accept yourself as you are. The more you feel accepted and acceptable, the more you are able to express yourself, act genuinely, and be fully present with others. We all want to belong, but we must be careful where and how we belong. When you are able to function well within a positive group, you will build self-esteem.

- Sense of Competence:

  This relates to how "good at things" and competent we feel. It is not perception or feeling that matters more than actual ability to accomplish a goal. If we interpret our experience as progress and/or success, we become more confident and more inclined to take risks in the future. Success breeds success. This sense of competency comes from achievement, taking risks that are beneficial, special talents, recognition of your talents by others, and other constructive feedback.

Characteristics of Low Self-Esteem

A person with low self-esteem will:

- Demean his/her own talents
- Feel that others don't value him
- Feel powerless
- Be easily influenced by others
- Express a narrow range of emotions
- Avoid situations that provoke anxiety
- Become defensive and easily frustrated

- Blame others for their own weaknesses

Low self-esteem has been linked with low life satisfaction, loneliness, anxiety, resentment, irritability, and depression. In other words, if you are not succeeding in anything, you will have low self-esteem.

CHARACTERISTICS OF HIGH SELF-ESTEEM

- Act independently
- Assume responsibility
- Be proud of accomplishments
- Approach new challenges with enthusiasm
- Exhibit a broad range of emotions
- Tolerate frustration well
- Feel capable of influencing others

High self-esteem has been correlated with academic success in high school, internal locus of control, high family outcome, and positive sense of self-attractiveness.

Desires Construct

Success is becoming extraordinary in areas of your life's desires. I remember lying in bed one day and made a decision to pursue a doctorate degree. It was a simple dream fourteen years ago that later became a reality. It would never have happened if I just laid there and dreamed it. I had to back up my belief with action. To live above the ordinary, one has to take extraordinary steps. You have to do what other people are not willing to do. I finished the master's program and years later completed the doctorate. I took classes during pregnancies, illnesses, hurts, pains, and major surgeries. I never took a leave of absence. It was not easy, but destiny is manifested one step at a time. Many don't believe that education matters. Our society has a high rate of high school and college dropouts. If education is a part of your existence, then destiny should be manifested in that area. Education is a means to an end. It is the forum through which minds and skills are developed. The Great Mandate in Genesis is to use the resources of this world to serve God and man. We serve mankind by developing our God-given talents and gifts. There is value in education.

So the question remains: who are you? Most of us define ourselves as mothers, wives, sisters, and friends. Women are relational in nature so these definitions are easy for us. We are naturally nurturing beings. The truth is that we are primarily spiritual beings with a nature that far surpasses our limited perspective. We are nurturers, but we are also creators. We are supernatural beings contained in a natural body. If we permit our nature to manifest, it will energize all areas of our lives—our souls and bodies. The revelation of our potent abilities will shatter our limited construction of self.

LIMITED CONSTRUCT

A limited construct view of self is based solely on external expectations, values, and validations. It derives its meaning from a deficient system of sustenance, the belief that there isn't enough for all of us to thrive. If we could only get enough to survive; if we could only provide for our families—be good wives, be good mothers, be good friends, etc. Don't speak in church; don't be too loud; don't draw attention to yourself. If we only knew how extraordinary we were, we wouldn't try to blend in so much. The difference between a moth and a butterfly is that one is mediocre and one is magnificent. Limited constructs of self are paradigms that have been set up in our lives due to our circumstances, experiences, and interactions. We find ourselves functioning within these constructs and manifesting limited success. Limited Construct says that I want to do better, but circumstances prevent me from excelling. Limited Construct gives power to the external sources. If our thoughts are patterned after the reality of our experiences, we deprive ourselves of the power to excel.

You are a limited construct thinker if you find yourself repeating the same negative dynamics of your surroundings. "I have a temper because my dad has a temper." "I can't go to college because no one in my family ever attended college." "It's okay to have a baby at sixteen because my mother had me at the age." "I don't need a man in my life." "I am miserable." "If it weren't for bad luck, I won't have any luck at all." "This is my ailment. This is my disease." "I cannot have what I want because I've been dealt a bad hand." "Look at me, I'm so ugly, so fat, so skinny, so unworthy." "I don't deserve better. They can't like me. They won't like me if they got to know me." "Life sucks. Why me? Woe is me." I could fill this book with all the limited construct statements that have crossed my path. Bad thoughts and actions never produce goodness.

Limited Construct women do not participate in their own lives. They have sold their birthrights like Esau in the book of Genesis. They do not have an understanding of themselves as complete women. They have denied the power of womanhood by operating in a sphere of helplessness. These are the women that I call *perpetual dependents*. These adult women still need a parent to sanction a thought, a husband to crystallize a dream, and others to give legitimacy to their humanity. These women cannot construct an original thought. They are too afraid of their own brilliance. They hide in the shadows of glory. They never take initiative and wait for the world to verify their existence. They suffocate in their loneliness and their desire for love strangles relationships.

These women are living in limbo, constantly waiting for their lives to begin. They want to become writers but refuse to pick up a pen; they want to become chefs but are too lazy to cook; they want a bachelor's degree but can't go to school. I call them *women in waiting*. They stay in abusive relationships. They are attracted to the opposite of hope. They are fearful and abusive. They extrapolate their inadequacies on others. They see faults and never praise the good in others. They are moms, wives, friends, sisters, but never lovers. They have submerged themselves in hopeless waters; having a form of godliness but denying the power. Their lives are dangerously ordinary. They inspire rebellion and chafe at rebuke. They always have an excuse for failure and put down success. They remain forever seedlings.

Jesus's parable about taking from the have-nots and giving it to the haves is quite significant. When it rains, it pours on the have-nots. Their lives are a constant torrent of disasters. They seem to wallow in shallow waters. We love them; we pity them and do for them. Some of us even keep them in the limited construct to satisfy our lofty view of self.

The image of a limited construct is never fully developed. They live perpetually in the shadow of destiny. They fill the graveyards with inscriptions that should read, "A woman in waiting, never really realized her life." There is no greater sadness in the heavens than to watch an ambassador of the kingdom perish in mediocrity. What happened to the reflection of glory and majesty?

CREATIVE CONSTRUCT

Creative construct is our ability to process the present reality with wisdom. This is the zone we enter during refinement of dreams. It is within this construct that we start the redemption of our souls by renewing our thought patterns. We are in creative construct when we reach beyond our limited understanding to a higher realm. When we operate in this realm, our ability is expanded by focusing on transcendent principles. The creative construct is a place of renewed perceptions. It could sometimes seem like the place we wrestle with our souls. Jacob wrestled with an angel all throughout the night, and by the morning dawn, he was a changed man with a new name and vision. During this time in our lives, we deal with soul issues like forgiveness and peace. We extend pardon and allow our souls to soar. We become conscious of the power to change and a quest for authenticity. We no longer shy from the difficult unknown because faith has moved our hearts to still waters. It is within this construct that we seek to believe and dream again. It is a place of hard work and suffering; it is also a place for rebirths and realizations.

The Apostle Paul encouraged the Philippians to work out their salvation with fear and trembling. The realization that victory is dependent on us can be a frightening. That this God Almighty in his sovereignty cannot simply snap a finger and change my circumstances is incomprehensible to some. That suffering and glory are intertwined .The road to the promise is paved with stones and concrete and pot holes and bumps. We stumble and fall; we endure the pain because our eternal eyes visualize the promise. These women can be bound up and oppressed in the earthly world, but they've attained freedom in their minds. You can't stop an unchained mind. The spirit of creative women allows them to draw from the waters of clarity.

    The psalmist's cry in his days of misery was to lift his eyes to a higher dimension. Creative people are hopeful and desire to become more than their present reality.

DESIRES FAITH

Faith is the super-ordinate principle through which all other biblical promises are realized. This is the one thread that binds all the great witnesses of generation past and present. The just will live by faith. (Habakkuk 2:4)

> Without faith it is impossible to please God, for he who comes to him must believe that He is and a rewarder of those that diligently seek him."
>
> Hebrews 11:6

- Faith will show you how to begin living beyond your shadow life. It is the power to unlocking your dreams.

- Faith will release you from mediocre to splendour.

- Faith will help you take care of emotional upheavals and sporadic attachments.

- Faith will set you on a course of emotional independence. You will become a leader within your world.

- Faith will unlock your transitory mindset. You will move from incompletes to completions.

- Faith will make you a powerful woman/wife/mother, thereby giving others around you permission to shine.

- Faith will show you how to tap into the under-utilized resources of your life.

- Faith can change your life by giving you more choices, more alternatives in the way you perceive yourself, live your life, and face your future.

DESIRE TO LOVE YOURSELF

Love thy neighbor as thyself.

Mark 12:31

The problem is that most of us do not have an intimate relationship with ourselves. We have become what other people think about us. Having an intimate self-relationship permits us intimate knowledge of how we function as individuals by examining the programs or paradigms that run our lives. Our greatest desire should be how to daily reflect excellence. Intimacy is about seeking and acknowledging the brilliance and the beauty of individuality. It is about learning to live in the moment of life without trepidation. A complete, intimate relationship with another person is only possible by achieving intimacy with self. Achieving personal relationship is about taking a leap of faith, daring to face the mirror, and owning the reflected image.

Permit the sunshine of your light to lead you to a place of personal wholeness. We all need assistance in understanding what is going on in our hearts and souls. We need to learn how to remain connected to ourselves in fundamental ways. We must understand the meaning of important life experiences and how to interpret them.

The *I Am* concept is divine. God revealed himself to Moses in the back of the wilderness as the "I Am." Thousands of years later, Jesus understood the power of I Am and tapped into its potency. He proclaimed himself as, I Am the resurrection and life; I Am the way, truth, and life; I Am the Bread of Life; I Am living water. You must declare who you are to become it. Are you living an *I Am* life? The *I Am* concept is a powerful and dynamic personal experience. It has the ability to transform the life of the person who grasps the meaning. *I Am* is not a focus on the characteristics or personalities of a person, it is simply to be present in any given situation of your life. *I Am* means that I am here at this very moment, enjoying all the pleasures and pains of my moment. It means that I choose to immense myself in the possibilities of my life.

We are desperately searching for someone else to give us permission when the most powerful moments are those we create ourselves. As we live every precious moment, we garner the powers of the physical and spiritual to become available to ourselves and others. I Am is proclaiming who you need in situations. When you feel like a failure, declare *I Am* Successful. When you feel lonely, declare *I Am* satisfied with friendships and love. When you feel weak, declare *I Am* strong.

Desires Prayers

Prayer is engaging the spirit in the affairs of life. The fundamental assumption is that you belong to both worlds. Remember that you are a spirit who lives in a body. You were sent to this earth as an ambassador of heaven; therefore, it is mandatory that you receive support from the heavenly headquarters. The scriptures acknowledge in Hebrews 12 that we have a city called the heavenly Jerusalem. The book of Hebrews, chapter 4 declares that we can boldly come to the "Throne of Grace," a place of mercy and truth. This is a place denied to women in the Old Testament, but now we can come boldly to the Father and be accepted. Prayer is accessing help from the heavenly city. We need God. We need the ministration of the angels, and we certainly need Jesus the mediator. Prayer is asking for divine intervention in the affairs of men. It is the medium for spiritual engagement. This means that you are responsible for your own salvation and those around you.

In prayer we find ourselves engaged in the restoration process. "Your will be done on earth as it is done in heaven." When we pray, we create life in places of decay; healing instead of disease; joy instead of sorrow; and freedom in place of prison. In prayer we engage the opposing forces until we win the battle. Jesus in the gospel of Luke 18:1 encourages us to choose prayer over anxiety. He went on to challenge his disciples to ask in order to receive. He cleaned out the temple and demanded that the house of God should be a place of prayer. In the New Testament, the Christian has become the house of God… The book of Corinthians posits that your body is the temple of the living God. We therefore can conclude that you must become a house of prayer. You are the center and home for prayer. You should always pray because it is your responsibility as Christian.

The disciples asked the master to teach them the art of prayer so we understand that there is a protocol. We can identify the fundamentals of prayer all throughout the scriptures. The foundational principle in the school of prayer is relational, that is, you must cultivate a relationship with the father.

"Our Father…"

If there is no connection to the Father, you do not have a place in the spirit. "I go to prepare a place…" Connection to the Father is what provides access into the spiritual kingdom. We build this relationship through spending time reading the scriptures and meditation. Become aware that there is another dimension to your existence, a God who is your father, Jesus who is pleading your case, angels who are ready to minister to you, and a great company of witnesses who are rooting for you.

The second and most vital principle in the school of prayer is to "hallow" his name or "honor" him. We give honor to whom honor is due. There is honor ascribed to presidents because of their position. If we believe that our God is the Lord of the earth, then we should approach his throne with praise. The Psalmist states, "I will enter his gates with thanksgiving in my heart into his courts with Praise."

A man of wisdom once said that it is to your advantage to select the biggest, wisest, greatest, and the most powerful God to serve. It is a pursuit in frustration if we choose to serve a being who is in need of assistance or who cannot answer your prayers. If our God is indeed the prayer answering one, then it makes sense to ascribe praise that is worthy to him. As parents, you know how it feels when your children appreciate your care and kindness. We treasure those moments when they demonstrate their appreciation for all that we do as parents. God appreciates when we appreciate him as a father. The Psalms is a good place to start.

Praise Outline

- Lord, you are so good to me

- Who is like my God among the earth

- You are the one who speaks, and the earth trembles

- You are God all by yourself

- You are the Ancient of Days

- The Ageless One

- The all powerful and almighty
- You are the source of all joy and power
- You are the miracle worker
- You are the way maker
- You are the God of breakthrough who makes a way where there is no way
- You are glorious and wonderful

The third principle of prayer we want to share is creating heaven on earth. The purpose of prayer is to create the will of the father on the earth. "Your will be done on earth as it is in heaven."

What we do in prayer is summon divine intervention on the basis of God's word because his word is his will.

The Bible is God's will, ratified by the blood of Jesus, and handed to the believer. If God has spoken it about you in the word, then it is your prerogative to claim it in prayer. You have the right to approach the throne of grace to plead your case.

One of the things we do in prayer is to present the will of God. Isaiah 41:12 asks us to bring a strong case before the LORD so that we are justified. You are like an attorney, presenting a case before the judge. An attorney worthy of his job would have researched the decisions made regarding other cases similar to the one he's presenting. When he comes before the judge, he is prepared and able to articulate why he should rule in his favor. In the same way, you should present your case to the LORD by stating why he should move on your behalf. Jesus, before the crowd gathered at the tomb of Lazarus, gave the Father a reason to demonstrate his power. "And I know that You always hear Me, but because of the people who are standing by I said this, that they may believe that You sent Me."

We have an adversary on earth whose purpose is to kill, steal your blessings, and destroy your destiny. He will forever be the accuser of the brethren, bringing faults before God and asking that you be condemned. We know that God is a righteous God, which means that people will automatically get what they deserve. He cannot break this spiritual principle, which is why the adversary has a litany of reasons why you should not have your prayers answered. You are the establishing witness for your life. Declare why you should be acquitted or granted your request. King Hezekiah prayed such a prayer in the book of Second Kings, chapter 20, when the king petitioned God based upon his past record to faithfulness. God later added fifteen more years to his life.

Prayer changes things, and it did for this king because he went before the LORD and pled his case. You can write your petition and read it to the LORD, as long as you have stated God's will as stated in the scriptures. Our God sits on a throne called grace which means that your judgment will be favorable. He asked that you come in the name of Jesus and with the scriptures relevant to the situation.

Search the scriptures until you discover yourself on the pages. You were on God's mind when the pages were being written, and it is of a surety that you are on those pages. Locate what the Bible says about your problems and the plan for your restoration.

Our next prayer principle is to abide in the spirit. Jesus's promise is that if we abide in him and his words abide in us, then prayers will be answered. The LORD is committed to answering your prayer when you stay rooted in his word. You need a connected heart to be a good warrior. "My son, give me your heart…" (Proverbs 23:26).

A fervent prayer comes from a connected heart. Don't allow your heart to lead you away from your place of blessing. There are people who pray long and hard, but because their hearts are disconnected from God, the prayers will remain unanswered. They might as well be reciting nursery rhymes. The heart is a powerful weapon in the school of prayer.

> For the eyes of the LORD run to and fro throughout the whole earth, to give strong support to those whose heart is blameless toward him.
>
> 2 Chronicles 16: 9

God is searching for sincere women who are not afraid to pray with unwavering belief that their prayers will be answered. The Apostle James chastised the double-minded because they are unstable in their requests and not able receive answers to their requests. Wavering in prayer can cause calamity for yourself and those depending on your faith. You should hold on to the Word used in prayer and not let it go. You will get your answers if you cannot be shaken. Faith is the expectation that your prayers will be answered.

Desires to Be Outside the Box

Rules are protective—nearly all the unexamined rules are lessons someone else has learned—as an attempt to protect us from a trauma that somebody else experienced.

Rules protect us from the unknown and sometimes keep us in the box of reality. The box is comfortable. Nelson Mandela's vacation home was an exact brick replica of the warden's house. When asked, he said it was pure pragmatism. He had grown accustomed to the floor plan and wanted a place where he could find the bathroom at night without stumbling in the dark.

Most of our boxes keep us safe because they are familiar.

Preserve our identity. The older we get, the more fixed our reality tends to be. Staying in the box means staying connected.

Most of us stay in the box to be "right."

All the benefits are valid. We do not have to chuck out everything from the past but simply in making committed choices that you can stand in and own. Simply looking at your world differently will put a crack in the box. Some rules you may want to keep. But you'll be keeping them because you want them.

Desires Declarations

A declaration is when we suddenly say, "It's not going that way anymore, and it's going like this." Declaring a new future isn't based on evidence. People who declare a new future without evidence are called heroes and visionaries, people who say, like Martin Luther King, "I have a dream;" who say, as Gandhi did, "India will be a free country without violence," etc. The beauty of declaration is that you don't need proof. It simply needs to be fueled by faith and actions to bring to reality.

You don't need the know-how, and you don't need permission. It is a declaration—nothing more, nothing less—that produces a breakthrough. In the absence of evidence, know-how, permission, or even courage, what a declaration does is push out a space of clearing for the possibility of a new reality. What you need for your declaration is simply a voice to speak and an ear to listen. It's only when you make a transaction with the outside world—an investment in something—that you have the possibility of gain. All you need to make a declaration is simply a voice and a listener. Declaration is what enables us to make the transition between our old, automatic results and the new futures we want to create.

Declare today who you will become tomorrow!

DESIRES POSSIBILITIES

What lights your fire? The ultimate result of exploring and pursuing your passion is that you create a whole new community for yourself.

1. What would others say are your talents, your distinctive competencies, your gifts?

2. What are some of your favorite ways of expressing yourself?

3. What are the things you like doing the most?

4. What things do you feel most strongly about?

5. What would you like to experience during this lifetime?

6. What is it you love?

7. What are you passionate about, even if you have no experience of it?

CREATING POSSIBILITIES

Get specific. Specificity is what enables others to understand your vision. The words used to declare your vision must be accurate, specific, and intentional. Your specific declaration connects you with others who are interested in your vision.

1. Narrow your declaration to a clear statement what you want to explore.

2. Engage people to assist you in generating possibilities.

3. Allow these participants to get really outrageous and go way outside the box of what they imagine possible.

4. Take note of their discourse.

5. Expand your vision.

6. Watch your world expand!

Create a Breakthrough Project

- Projects must be compelling. You must feel exuberant at the very thought of it? If not, is there a way to frame it so you'd be more passionate about it?

- It must be somewhere between highly improbable and nearly impossible. If not, think bigger, something that you think would just be absolutely, dazzlingly, terrifying wonderful.

- Can you stand that it's at least possible? If not, scale back, but just enough so that you can admit it's not impossible.

- Is your breakthrough project stated positively and empowering? If not, reword your inspiring challenge so that it is.

- Is it specific? Have you stated a specific date by which you'll achieve that result? Pick a date between three and eighteen months away that makes you uneasy and excited but not horribly uncomfortable.

THE MOUNTAINTOP BLUEPRINT

Starting from the top and looking down.

1. Ask someone to record your pathways for you, so that you can be fully present.

2. On a big piece of paper, draw a simple dotted-line diagram of a mountain. Put it up on the wall.

3. Now, state your breakthrough project to your group—what you'll do and by when you'll do it. Write your goal and your deadline at the top of the mountain.

4. As part of registering your accomplishment, describe the celebration you're going to have. Then ask your group to answer the question: What would have happened just before that to

allow for that? Keep asking question until the group brings you back to the present.

5. Design at least two pathways to your breakthrough result so you can't get stuck in the "there's only one way of getting there" mentally.

6. Give yourself a day to create an action plan from all the possibilities you gathered. Then assign your deadline!

Desires to Plant a Speaking Seed

What is a seed? It is the container of life, but it is not useful until it is released into the right soil. The law of seed and harvest is a common theme in the Bible. "As long as the earth endures, seedtime and harvest…will never cease."

We must release that which we desire the most. It is human nature to self-protect or conserve what is left especially when it looks like lack is inevitable. But in order to be restored, you must release that which you seek the most. In your thirst for love, you must sow love; in desperation for financial breakthrough, you must give your last; in the desire for a child, you must become a caretaker. The earth has been programmed to react to this principle. The book of Ecclesiastes 11 tells us to, "Cast your bread upon the waters, for after many days you will find it again."

Then there is what can be considered speaking seed. This is the type that gets attention in the spirit realm, and it usually results in a miracle. "For the life of the flesh is in the blood: and I have given it to you upon the altar to make an atonement for your souls: for it is the blood that maketh an atonement for the soul," (Lev. 17:11).

Miracles are heavenly intervention in earthly matters. This type of seed costs everything. You have literally poured out yourself, and it has cost you everything. Your desire for restoration should be all consuming. These are offerings in the genre of the ancient sacrifices that command the hands of the God. "…the blood is the life" (Deut. 12:23). "Out of the heart are the issues of life" (Prov. 4:23).

This type of seed cost you dearly, but it shows total dependence on the LORD. Your seed basically tells him that you are laying down your life in exchange for his. You have poured it all on the altar of his divine grace. We also understand that blood speaks. "…and to the sprinkled blood that speaks a better word than the blood of Abel" (Heb. 12: 24b).

The speaking seed is what you want when you are in between a rock and a hard place because it will keep speaking in the presence of the Father. It is blood seed, and it has no choice but to speak. It is a divine principle. I particularly like the story of the Prophet Elijah's commanding a miracle. The nation of Samaria had not seen rain for at least three years and six months because of the evil of King Ahab and a nation who had adopted evil. Elijah staged a contest of sort between his God and Baal. The one who answered by fire should be worthy of the people's allegiance. "The god who answers by fire—he is God."

The Baal prophets could not get their gods to respond, even though they had built the altar of sacrifice. Elijah did something that was quite significant when it was his turn. Then he said to them,

> "Fill four large jars with water and pour it on the offering and on the wood."
>
> "Do it again," he said, and they did it again.
>
> "Do it a third time," he ordered, and they did it the third time.
>
> The water ran down around the altar and even filled the trench.

Elijah offered to the Lord the most sacred thing in the land: water. Remember everyone needed water, because it had not rained in three-and-a-half years. Elijah had learned the secret of a speaking seed. At that moment, the only thing to get the attention of a mighty God was to offer that which was precious and sacred. I guarantee that the people cried against Elijah as he ordered the water to be poured in the trench. But Elijah knew he must command the heavens by offering that which was most precious. Contrary to common belief, God is not monitoring the affairs of men daily because He is not a micromanager. "The highest heavens belong to the Lord, but the earth he has given to man" (Psalm 115:16).

God expects human beings to take control and establish this earth. God blessed them and said to them, "Be fruitful and increase in number; fill the earth and subdue it" (Gen. 1: 28).

Now one of the ways to call for a miracle is by offering speaking seed. Then heaven invades earth. That was what the prophet did. He offered God the seed that would speak the loudest. Elijah received his miracle when His God answered by fire! He also commanded the heavens to open, and rain fell as never before.

You can be restored if you would offer this type of offering. What is it that you need? A few years ago, my family was in deep financial trouble. Basically, we had lost almost everything. I didn't have a stable income, and things looked pretty dismal. I was moved to sow the last money that we had in the account. There was nothing left to do. I knew this money was all we had, but I also knew that keeping it would do us no good. I remember withdrawing all of it from the bank, and I got on my knees, sobbing before God, knowing that we might not have anything to eat the next week. I released that money into someone's ministry by faith. Almost immediately things began to happen. We started getting job offers to the point that we turned some down. My seed turned into a speaking seed, telling the Father, "You have to intervene now because it's a life for a life. The gift is from her heart, and I am speaking miracle harvest for this family." A man of God, Charles Capps, once said that, "If you are down to your last dollar, don't spend it, sow it. Then it becomes significant. If it doesn't meet your need, turn it into a seed."

You have cried enough for yourself, find someone else who is in a worse situation and heal them with your tears. After you have sown your significant seed, thank and wait expectantly for the next step. He will give you directions or instructions on how to receive the miracle. And like Mary told the disciple, "Whatever he tells you to do, do it!"

Become single-minded about following instructions. Singleness is the supreme and ultimate intention of the mind. Focus your attention, and it will affect your intentions, which will affect your commitment that will ultimately release your miracle. Believe in the seeds of that you sow whether they are financial, relational, or whatever type of love seed sown—if you plant, it will grow.

Confession

Lord, I speak your word, according to Isaiah 55:11, that the words that are released today will not return to you without fulfilling its purpose. Psalm 112 says that my generation is blessed because I am righteous—wealth and riches reside in my house. I deal graciously and lend, and I guide my affairs with discretion.

Psalm 126 tells me that he who goes forth weeping and bearing seed will doubtlessly come back rejoicing and bringing her harvest. I declare that all the seeds of love, trust, forgiveness, desires, and generosity that I have sown, even in tears, will become harvest time in my life.

Like the woman of Zarephath who gave her significant seed after hearing the word; like the widow whose mite caught Jesus's attention; I have sown my significant seed and believe that I receive a bountiful reward in Jesus's name.

Lord, I thank you for my seed speaks as it bursts into harvest.

I declare that I have sown bountifully, and I believe that I will have a bountiful harvest. According to Proverbs 11:25, "The generous soul will be made rich, and he who waters will also be watered himself." Therefore, I make a demand on this word to work for me. I am watered back in all my ways. I am restored because of my generosity. I do not have any areas of lack in the name of Jesus.

The blessing of 2 Corinthians 9:8 is working for me, and I will always and under all circumstance possess enough to require no aid or support and furnished in abundance for every good work and charitable donation. I am made whole!

Desires to Understand Personality Types

There is probably no more difficult and painful emotion than shame. Shame involves complete self-condemnation. It is a major attack against the self in which the individual believes that they will be found utterly unacceptable by society. As a result of its overwhelming force, shame causes feelings of disgrace and dishonor. A person who feels shame wants to hide from everyone. By contrast, guilt does not involve self-condemnation. Instead, guilt involves self-criticism for a mistaken act or behavior. The self-criticism is directed at an error that one has committed for which they feel guilty and want to make restoration. Of course, there is overlap between shame and guilt where the shamed person may also have feelings of guilt. However, a shamed person says I am wrong while the guilty says I did something wrong. The former implies that she is damaged while the latter simply regrets doing wrong.

Shame is much more public than guilt. A person who feels shame expects condemnation from everyone.

The person who feels guilt may be the only one who is aware that an error has been committed. A guilty person may feel a loss of self-esteem but not to the extent that is experienced by the shamed individual. For example, a student who successfully cheats on an examination may feel guilty for the high grade the professor has awarded because it was not earned. But no one is aware of the cheating. On the other hand, a student who is caught cheating during an exam, with books open on his lap, right in front of his fellow students, may indeed feel extreme shame and embarrassment. The shame is due to the fact that everyone is aware of the serious nature of the infraction.

In the great American novel *The Scarlett Letter* by Nathanial Hawthorne, Hester Prynne exemplifies the power of shame. The novel takes place in puritanical Boston during the seventeenth century. As the novel points out, there was a scaffold in the center of Boston where sinners were publicly displayed. Towns-people would hurl insults at them to humiliate them for having sinned. Hester suffered this fate when it was discovered that her child was the product of an adulterous affair. She was sentenced to wear a large scarlet letter (A) on her breast. She was socially isolated and alienated for her indiscretion.

SOCIAL AVOIDANCE

There are a significant number of people who suffer from the personality disorder called *social avoidance*. Social avoidance disorder is sometimes mistaken for social anxiety disorder or social phobia. The difference between an anxiety disorder or social phobia and an avoidant personality disorder has to do with the nature of personality disorders. A personality disorder is a lifelong pattern of behavior that causes problems with work and personal relationships. The fact that this is a lifelong pattern of behavior makes treatment extremely difficult. The symptoms of avoidant personality disorder include lifelong patterns of behavior such as:

1. Social phobia with enormous anxiety about being around other people.

2. Extreme shyness.

3. Feelings of inadequacy and sensitivity to rejection and criticism.

4. Choosing loneliness and isolation instead of risking connecting to other people.

5. Extreme sensitivity to criticism and shame when criticized.

6. Avoiding criticism more than anything else.

7. Choosing social isolation as a way to avoid criticism.

8. Avoiding making eye contact at work or elsewhere.

9. Avoiding saying anything.

The avoidant individual is on the lookout for any signs of disapproval from others. This type of vigilant appraisal of others may even have a paranoid flavor to it but has more to do with the overpowering wish to protect themselves against ridicule, derision, and humiliation.

Shame and Its Relation to the Avoidant Personality

While shame is a universal human emotion found in all civilizations and cultures, there are different set of roots from which the reasons for shame spring. Here in Western civilization, there is a lot of emphasis placed on being a separate, autonomous, unemotional individualist. Hollywood movies with actors such as Clint Eastwood, John Wayne, and Gary Cooper portray the heroic male who is strong, courageous, and silent. These roles portray self-reliance to the utmost degree.

The high value placed on individuality and self-sufficiency in Western society plays a significant role in complicating things for those who struggle with avoidant personality disorder. The complication is that the value placed on individuality becomes a rationalization or excuse for avoiding social interaction. For these individuals, social interaction is so painful that it must be shunned at all costs. Yet, in most careers it is necessary to behave in socially acceptable ways in order to become successful. It soon becomes apparent to these individuals that they must rely on the cooperation of other people in the work place and elsewhere. Needing the cooperation of others at work is experienced as a threat because they are forced to face up to their social fears and long-established patterns of behavior. In fact, the socially avoidant person may experience having to rely on others as a humiliation. Strongly invested in the belief that it is better to "go it alone," they want to withdraw into isolation. It's a real conundrum to want to avoid social contact on the one hand because it arouses too much anxiety and to have to admit to needing others in order to function successfully. Independence is highly valued regardless of issues of anxiety and the need for social avoidance. At the very same time, the nature of the socially avoidant person is such that any criticism, even the slightest, is experienced as acutely painful. In fact, being criticized causes the avoidant person to feel humiliated and, therefore, shamed.

The Need to Belong

The simple fact is that all of us, as members of the human species, have a need to belong. While most of us need to spend some time alone, too much aloneness results in depression. Even those with avoidant personality disorder become depressed if they are alone too much of the time. The healthy need to feel accepted and to belong outweighs the wish to avoid.

In all of the cases of avoidant personality disorder, the individuals were either married or in long-term relationships. In addition, most were working or had been working until they were forced to resign as a result of overwhelming anxiety and severe depression. Some are extremely bright and have attained high levels of education and professional status. They ran into trouble quickly after they started their careers as a result of the demand put on them to be social in their job or profession. As a result of this trouble, they were forced to seek psychotherapy.

Of the cases of people with avoidant personality disorder, those who were married also ran into difficulty with their spouses. The reasons for the marital difficulties had to do with the fact that the spouse with the personality disorder rarely wanted to go out and socialize. The unwillingness to be in social situations even included going to movies, restaurants, and having friends and family over for social visits.

Treatment

There are a variety of treatments available for avoidant personality disorder. Medication can be useful in reducing anxiety and depression. Among the types of medications used are the anti-depressants and/or the anti-anxiety drugs. When these symptoms are reduced, individuals with this disorder often find it easier to make use of psychotherapy.

Cognitive-behavioral therapy is most useful with the social phobias and avoidant disorders because the emphasis is on changing thinking patterns as well as modifying behavior. The emphasis is on helping the patient face and become desensitized to the stimuli (social situations) that cause them the most trouble. Behavior modification includes learning the social skills necessary to function in society. Among the skills needed to be developed are:

1. Making eye contact with people.

2. Learning to greet people with a smile and rehearsing common verbal interactions between people.

3. Learning how to be assertive in ways that are appropriate.

4. Learning what to say or how to respond in a variety of social situations.

5. Learning and rehearsing how to carry on common, everyday conversations with people.

Attending assertive training classes is something that can also be helpful for these individuals, as is group therapy and learning the social skills necessary to function in society.

OTHER HEALING MEDICINE AND THERAPIES

Functional mood-enhancing therapies:

- Diet and depression, anxiety and stress options: food allergy elimination diet, Candida diet, anti-inflammation diet, increased intake of colored fruits and vegetables, dairy elimination, gluten elimination, detoxification diet, well-balanced diet

- Minerals that can augment stress, depression, and anxiety treatments: minerals-zinc, magnesium; Vitamins-B12, B6, thiamine, folic acid; other supplements: S-adenosyl methionine (same), inositol

- Herbal contributions to stress management techniques: St. John's Wort, kava, ashwaganda, ginseng, ginkgo

- Bio-Behavioral approaches as stress management techniques: appropriate exercise,

- better sleep, repairing disordered breathing, relaxation skills (e.g. guided visual imagery), instant stress reduction techniques (e.g. freeze frame)
- Others components of natural depression treatments, stress relief, and anxiety improvement: fish oil, borage/primrose oil, inositol, phosphatidyly serine, CDP-choline, DNA/RNA mixes, trimethyl glycine, L-Carnitine, Acetyl-L-Carnitin, tryptophan, 5-hydroxy tryptophan, tyrosine, phenylalanine, GABA

Alternative treatments for depression, stress management techniques, and natural anxiety treatments can make a big difference in your life.

Functional medicine views all systems of the mind and body as part of one large interactive web. This implies that any obstacle to healing that affects on part of the system feeds through and harms all others. Any improvement we can make in any part is also likely to feed through this web and improve your well-being as a whole.

Acupuncture is based on the ancient Chinese belief that there is a universal life energy called "Qi" (or Chi) that circulates throughout the body along pathways called meridians. When this energy flows freely, we experience good health. If energy flow is blocked, the system is disrupted, and pain and illness can occur. Acupuncture uses fine needles to stimulate meridian points on the body to free up the Qi energy and restore normal functions and balance to the body. Don't be stumped by the Qi and Chi; all powers belong to our God.

Chiropractic medicine is a system of healthcare that focuses on the self-healing capacity of the body and the importance of proper nervous system function as a key to maintaining good health. Chiropractic therapy commonly uses spinal manipulation to restore proper function to musculoskeletal systems; it may also include lifestyle modification, nutritional therapy, physiotherapy, and other modalities.

Family medicine is a medical practice that supports children, adolescents, and adults for a wide range of general health conditions, as well as preventive care.

Massage therapy is a hands-on therapy that manipulates the body's muscular and soft tissue structure through a variety of techniques that help to increase range of motion and flexibility, reduce stress and pain, improve circulation, and support overall well-being. Common massage modalities include Swedish, Shiatsu, trigger point, deep tissue, hot stone therapy, and more.

Naturopathic medicine is a distinct method of primary health care—an art, science, philosophy, and practice of diagnosis, treatment, and prevention of illness. Naturopathic physicians seek to restore and maintain optimum health in their patients by emphasizing the body's inherent self-healing process. This is accomplished through education and the use of natural therapeutics. Naturopathic treatment often uses a blend of therapies that may include any of the following: nutritional substances, botanical medicine, homeopathy, naturopathic physical manipulative therapy, minor surgery, natural childbirth, psychotherapy, and acupuncture.

EEG-based biofeedback for the brain, accessing the brain's own built-in mechanism for self-healing and optimal functioning. Neurofeedback is a revolutionary way to work with the brain using a reliable well known tool in an entirely new way. It is a gentle, non-invasive permanent brain wave therapy for ADD/ADHD, post-traumatic stress, anxiety, insomnia, traumatic brain injury, learning disabilities, autism spectrum disorder, addiction/substance abuse, panic disorder, OCD, social anxiety, and more. This therapy typically includes nutritional and supplementary treatment to optimize brain function.

A behavioral therapy that helps people learn how to consciously control involuntary conditions such as muscle spasms or migraines. Biofeedback uses painless electrodes on the body to monitor biological functions (e.g., heart rate, skin temperature, blood pressure, breathing rate) and provide feedback to the patient as they perform relaxation or visualization techniques to bring about a desired change. The biofeedback device reports progress by a change in beeps or flashes or tones.

Nutrition therapy focuses on restoring and maintaining optimal health through carefully managed diet plans that address the patient's nutritional needs.

Therapies for skin and face include cosmeceutical-grade facial products (such as Skin Medica) and chemical peels. Cosmeceuticals are physician-dispensed, non-prescription skin care products designed to enhance skin appearance, reduce signs of aging, and provide other skin care benefits. Chemical peels give your skin a more youthful look and will improve brown discolorations and blemishes, acne, fine wrinkles, and sun-damaged skin on the face and neck. The peeling process exfoliates the skin and enhances the skin's ability to produce collagen. Chemical peels must be done under the supervision of a medical doctor and are not available at spas. A series of peels is recommended for best results. (Insurance is often not accepted for this service.)

Sound healing is a form of therapy that uses sound to balance and align the physical body and its energy centers. It works on the premise that everything in the universe is energy in vibration, and that using various types of sound, healing can occur when the body is realigned to its natural frequencies of vibration. Practitioners may use intuition, intention, and visualization to select appropriate sound-healing frequencies, and therapy might include human voice, tuning forks, tonal sounds, or music to help release pain and stress, and align unbalanced areas of the body. Our God is the author of sounds. Clapping, singing, drums and all types of instruments are healing tools.

Psychotherapy
- Psychotherapy helps people live well-adjusted lives.

- Understand the behaviors, emotions, and ideas that contribute to his or her illness or maladaptive behaviors.

- It is not only for people with a mental illness. I believe that we can all benefit from some form of therapy.

- Understand and identify the life problems or events—a major illness, a death in the family, a loss of a job, or a divorce—that contribute to their issues and help them understand which aspects of those problems they may be able to solve or improve.

- Regain a sense of control and pleasure in life.

- Learn coping techniques and problem-solving skills.

Therapy can be given in a variety of formats, including:

- Individual: This therapy involves only the patient and the therapist.

- Group: Two or more patients may participate in therapy at the same time. Patients are able to share experiences and learn that others feel the same way, and have had the same experiences.

- Marital/couples: This type of therapy helps spouses and partners understand why their loved one has these challenges, what changes in communication and behaviors can help, and what they can do to cope.

- Family: Because family is a key part of the team that helps the client get better, it is sometimes helpful for family members to understand what their loved one is going through, how they themselves can cope, and what they can do to help.

While therapy can be done in different formats—family, group, and individual—there are also several different approaches that mental health professionals can take to provide therapy. After talking with the patient about their situations, the therapist will decide which approach to use based on the suspected underlying factors contributing to the condition. Different approaches to therapy include:

Psychodynamic therapy is based on the assumption that the clients problems stem from unresolved, generally unconscious conflicts often stemming from childhood. The goal of this type of therapy is for the patient to understand and cope better with these feelings by talking about the experiences. Psychodynamic therapy is administered over a period of three to four months, although it can last longer, even years.

Interpersonal therapy focuses on the behaviors and interactions a patient has with family and friends. The primary goal of this therapy is to improve communication skills and increase self-esteem during a short period of time. It usually lasts three to four months and works well for depression caused by mourning, relationship conflicts, major life events, and social isolation.

Psychodynamic and interpersonal therapies help patients resolve mental illness caused by:

- Loss (grief)

- Relationship conflicts

- Role transitions (such as becoming a mother or a caregiver)

Cognitive-behavioral treatment counseling (CBT) is a highly effective practical stress management technique than can be learned very quickly. It often does wonders. CBT is very different from standard psychotherapies, emphasizing practical skills for handling stresses and not over-reacting. Most people who are ill tend to fall into frustration's mental traps—making mountains out of molehills, seeing the glass half-empty, feeling helpless, and losing hope. Fortunately, once we realize how this happens, we can quickly master simple mental tricks that quickly put our thoughts and feelings into a more constructive mode.

CBT stress management techniques are not a substitute for standard psychotherapy. Its techniques are different. However, CBT stress management techniques can make standard therapy more effective. Indeed, even people who don't require therapy but who are struggling to cope with an illness often find benefit from even a few sessions of training in CBT stress management techniques.

Christian therapy should be transcendent therapy that teaches us the divine principles of wellness. It is not about preaching the gospel but rather treating your brokenness with healing leaves of truth and strategies. It is God's will for us to be restored, and the Christian therapist should prepare an environment conducive to healing and have the skills to administer treatment. Some ministers do not believe in getting trained but imagine visiting a doctor who did not take the time to hone his/her skills through the right medical school. The Christian therapist should have a sound theology and skilled practitioner. Christian therapy should emphasize the centrality of spirit while allowing the client to reconnect.

Therapy works best when you attend all of your scheduled appointments. The effectiveness of therapy depends on your active participation. It requires time, effort, and regularity. As you begin therapy, establish some goals with your therapist. Then spend time periodically reviewing your progress with your therapist. If you don't like your therapist's approach or if you don't think the therapist is helping you, talk to him or her about it, and seek a second opinion if both you and your therapist agree. Don't discontinue therapy abruptly.

Here are some tips to use when starting therapy for the first time:

- Identify sources of stress: Try keeping a journal and note stressful as well as positive events.

- Restructure priorities: emphasize positive, effective behavior.

- Make time for recreational and pleasurable activities.

- Communicate: Explain and assert your needs to someone you trust; write in a journal to express your feelings.

- Try to focus on positive outcomes and finding methods for reducing and managing stress.

Remember, therapy involves evaluating your thoughts and behaviors, identifying stresses that contribute to your condition, and working to modify both. People who actively participate in therapy recover more quickly and have fewer relapses. Also, keep in mind therapy is treatment that addresses specific causes of illness or disorders; it is not a "quick fix." It takes longer to begin to work than medication, but there is evidence to suggests that its effects last longer. Medication may be needed immediately in cases of severe mental illness, but the combination of therapy and medicine is very effective.

DESIRES *I Am*

The *I Am* concept is powerful and dynamic. It has the ability to change the lives. *I Am* is not simply a focus on the characteristics or personalities of a person; it is simply to be present in the here and now. *I Am* means that I am here at this very moment, enjoying all the benefits and feeling all the pain of this moment. It means that I chose to immense myself in the possibilities and adversities of this moment. We have been taught to look forward to tomorrow but living is for *today*. Your life at this moment is the reality, and it is the best that you can do for this moment. Embrace it; enrich it, and enjoy it!

I Am is the ability to be alone with your spouse, children, and friends without barriers.

I Am is the ultimate surrender without pretense.

I Am means owning this moment.

I Am concept is powerful and dynamic. It has the ability to change the lives.

I Am is not simply a focus on the characteristics or personalities of a person; it is simply to be present.

I Am means that you are here enjoying all the benefits and feeling all the pain of this moment.

I Am means that you chose to immense yourself in the possibilities and adversities of the present.

WRITING YOUR *I Am*

I Am
I am (two special characteristics).
I wonder (something you are actually curious about).
I hear (an imaginary sound).
I see (an imaginary sight).
I want (an actual desire).
I am (the first line of the poem restated).
I pretend (something you actually pretend to do).
I feel (a feeling about something imaginary).
I touch (an imaginary touch).
I worry (something that really bothers you).
I cry (something that makes you very sad).
I am (the first line of the poem repeated).
I understand (something you know is true).
I say (something you believe in).
I dream (something you actually dream about).
I try (something you really make an effort about).
I hope (something you actually hope for).
I am (the first line of the poem repeated).

I Ams

I am beautifully and wonderfully created.
I am positively ravishing.
I am radiant.
I am a sweet wife/husband.
I am a loving wife/husband.
I am successful.
I am wealthy beyond imagination.
I am confident.
I am admired.
I am beautiful.
I am delightful.
I am free to excel.
I am positive.
I am brilliant.
I am at peace.
I am stress free.
I am wonderful.
I am present.
I am loving.

Make a list of your own *I AMs*, and say it to yourself daily then watch for the changes.

LIVING DESIRES PLAN

Most women have never taken inventory of their life. You can't build a house without a plan so also one cannot build a life without a blueprint. *Living Desires* is a purposeful life plan designed to help you live a balanced and fulfilled life. It uses a form of expressive writing, personal and informal, written to encourage comprehension and reflection on the part of the writer.

Living Desires is a form of practical reasoning that consists of finding causes for the outcomes one wants, but it may also involve scheduling or picking one among the various options that would achieve one's goals.

Define Yourself

How do you define yourself? Have you gone through life defining yourself by what you do rather than who you are? The most common conversation starter in our society is: What do you do? We are then forced to label ourselves, and we become business owners, educators, bankers, doctors, managers, etc. The problem with this mode of thinking is that you define yourself based on physical things instead of intrinsic values. Changes in circumstances could then lead to an identity crisis. You should learn how to define yourself by your uniqueness. What makes you the special human being that you are; what separates you from other people around you? Having a good understanding of the person within lays a foundation for success in the world.

You should understand who you are because of what I call identity collision and personality mergers. Sometimes we get so comfortable in our context that we start to adapt other people's beliefs and purposes. It is therefore imperative to have a complete understanding of what differentiates you from others in order to build an effective life.

Take a moment now to shine a light on who you are. Make a list of your top ten qualities. We are all unique individuals, because we have qualities that distinguish us from others. My qualities are assertive or bossy, insightful, nice, hardworking, ambitious, tenacious, loner, impatient, flamboyant, and personable. Each of you will make a list of your qualities and characteristics.

WHO ARE YOU? FEMALE

1.
2.
3.
4.
5.
6.
7.
8.
9.
10.

IDENTIFY YOUR TALENTS AND GIFTS

Some of us have gifts and talents that cannot be overlooked. A talent is natural ability. You might be a talented writer, teacher, basketball player, singer, artist, manager, etc. Sometimes our talents and gifts are windows to the higher purpose. We should learn to identify them. If you cannot use your talent or gift to fulfill your purpose then you shouldn't turn it into a career. It should stay a hobby. Maybe you're a good basketball player and you would like to use that avenue to create wealth in order for you to help the unfortunate people.

Allen Iverson, the basketball player, had to turn pro because of the abject poverty of his family. His sister needed a specialist for her medical problem, his mother's apartment was leaking sewage, and his stepdad was an unemployed convict. Allen had a talent that had to be utilized for the benefit of the family. Do not get stuck with playing basketball for the rest of your life when your real purpose is to bring healing or relief to others. Our gifts and talents should propel us to higher heights. It should bring goodwill to your family and the world.

Talents and Gifts

Make a list of your gifts and talents.

1.

2.

3.

4.

5.

Ever feel like your goals just don't inspire you to take action? Is the one thing you remember when you reach your goal how hard it was to get there? Then your goals may not be *SMART*! *SMART* is an acronym for goals that are: specific, measurable, attainable, relevant, and time-based.

A specific goal is simple and easy to describe. When you set goals for yourself, are they specific and precise? "I want to be happy" is not specific. "I want to live happily in Hawaii" is specific. Your personal power lies in clarity.

A measurable goal is one that has a specific outcome. How will you know when you've achieved your goal? If someone were to videotape you reaching your goal, would it be obvious whether you achieved your goal or not? For example, the goal of saving $10,000 in a year is measurable. On December 31st, you have either reached the goal or not. It can be easily measured.

An attainable goal is one that allows you to stretch but is not impossible. Let's say you want to make a million dollars. Great goal. But, if you are currently out of work or are not saving money, this goal is currently not achievable. If financial prosperity is a goal, start by getting work or saving/investing, and then move on to the next attainable goal as you work toward your vision.

A relevant goal is one that has meaning for you. It is not just a good idea or a *should*. It reflects who you are and what you value as a human being. Pick something that gives you joy. If you want to lose weight, connect that desire to a larger intention. Living a healthy and fit life is the larger intention that makes the weight loss goal relevant. Choose things that are important to *you* and that make a difference in your life.

A time-based goal is one that has an end date. Even if you don't know if you can accomplish your goal in the time you've set for yourself, set a date anyway. The mind responds to specifics. Setting a date and creating a plan or path for the goal will notify your mind you mean business!

One of the reasons that goal setting has such a bad reputation is that we often confuse a goal with a task. If you don't experience a resounding *yes* as you create goals for yourself, then you are creating tasks. You are creating another variation of a to-do list. Ask yourself: Will I be relieved when it is done? If the answer is yes to this question, you have a task, not a goal.

Ask yourself: What do I truly want? What is really important to me? Look at what you gravitate toward naturally. This is a great place to start making SMART goals. Remember, goals are part of the process that moves you toward your dreams.

GOALS

- Spiritual:
- Emotional:
- Family:
- Career:
- Physical:
- Social:
- Financial:

Action Plan

The Big Picture

What are some of the things you need to do to accomplish your hopes and dreams?

1.

2.

3.

4.

5.

6.

7.

The Roadblocks to Success

Most people never get to the simple steps of an action plan leading to goals because of common obstacles that get in the way. Making assumptions will stop a dream dead in its tracks. You'll know you've come up against this roadblock when you hear yourself say things like: I'd really love to get a new job, but I'll never be able to make the kind of money I make now. I'd like to be in an intimate relationship, but it will be so difficult to find someone at my age. I'd love to start my own business, but I'll never get the funding.

Why not give your dreams a fighting chance! When you make negative assumptions, you give you power away to fears and concerns that may not even turn out to be valid. Bet on yourself, and you will succeed. It's easy to think that the fear we feel when starting out will stay with us, or even worse, increase over time. But, with every positive step in the right direction, your courage muscles get stronger. And here's another important thing to know: excitement neutralizes fear. As you take action to fulfill your dreams, every success that you experience, big or small, will fuel your enthusiasm to forge ahead and accomplish even more challenging goals. With this enthusiasm in place, you'll work your way through challenges with more ease. For example, if you finally decide to go back to school, you'll probably find that your excitement about learning something that's of interest to you will outweigh the heavy load of homework you were worried about handling in the beginning.

THE DETAILS

Someone once said, "Love is in the details." Details tell the other person that you care enough to notice specific things about them. Detail is selecting the blue blouse for your wife because you know that's what she likes. Details show that we care for each other so plan your lives intricately.

You will design yearly plans for your life.

Action Plans for Year One

Spiritual

1.

2.

3.

Emotional

1.

2.

3.

Family

1.

2.

3.

Career

1.

2.

3.

Physical

1.

2.

3.

Social

1.

2.

3.

Financial

1.

2.

3.

List Some of Your Roadblocks and Solutions

Obstacle:

1.

2.

3.

Soul Desires

Solution:

1.

2.

3.

Obstacle:

1.

2.

3.

Solution:

1.

2.

3.

Obstacle:

1.

2.

3.

Solution:

1.

2.

3.

Obstacle:

1.

2.

3.

Solution:

1.

2.

3.

Achievements

This is where you list the things you achieved this year. Don't get discouraged if everything on your list wasn't accomplished; simply carry them over to the next year. Way to go!

This is to certify that I, _____, accomplished the following during year one_____:

1.

2.

3.

4.

5.

6.

7.

Action Plans for Year Two

Spiritual

1.

2.

3.

Emotional

1.

2.

3.

Family

1.

2.

3.

Career

1.

2.

3.

Physical

1.

2.

3.

Social

1.

2.

3.

Financial

1.

2.

3.

List Some of Your Roadblocks and Solutions

Obstacle:

1.

2.

3.

Soul Desires

Solution:

1.

2.

3.

Obstacle:

1.

2.

3.

Solution:

1.

2.

3.

Obstacle:

1.

2.

3.

Solution:

1.

2.

3.

Obstacle:

1.

2.

3.

Solution:

1.

2.

3.

Achievements

This is where you list the things you achieved this year. Don't get discouraged if everything on your list wasn't accomplished; simply carry them over to the next year. Way to go!

This is to certify that I, _____, accomplished the following during year two_____:

1.

2.

3.

4.

5.

6.

7.

Action Plans for Year Three

Spiritual

1.

2.

3.

Emotional

1.

2.

3.

Family

1.

2.

3.

Career

1.

2.

3.

Physical

1.

2.

3.

Social

1.

2.

3.

Financial

1.

2.

3.

List Some of Your Roadblocks and Solutions

Obstacle:

1.

2.

3.

Soul Desires

Solution:

1.

2.

3.

Obstacle:

1.

2.

3.

Solution:

1.

2.

3.

Obstacle:

1.

2.

3.

Solution:

1.

2.

3.

Obstacle:

1.

2.

3.

Solution:

1.

2.

3.

Achievements

This is where you list the things you achieved this year. Don't get discouraged if everything on your list wasn't accomplished; simply carry them over to the next year. Way to go!

This is to certify that I, _____, accomplished the following during year three_____:

1.

2.

3.

4.

5.

6.

7.

ACTION PLANS FOR YEAR FOUR

Spiritual

1.

2.

3.

Emotional

1.

2.

3.

Family

1.

2.

3.

Career

1.

2.

3.

Physical

1.

2.

3.

Social

1.

2.

3.

Financial

1.

2.

3.

List Some of Your Roadblocks and Solutions

Obstacle:

1.

2.

3.

Solution:

1.

2.

3.

Obstacle:

1.

2.

3.

Solution:

1.

2.

3.

Obstacle:

1.

2.

3.

Solution:

1.

2.

3.

Obstacle:

1.

2.

3.

Solution:

1.

2.

3.

Achievements

This is where you list the things you achieved this year. Don't get discouraged if everything on your list wasn't accomplished; simply carry them over to the next year. Way to go!

This is to certify that I, _____, accomplished the following during year four_____:

1.

2.

3.

4.

5.

6.

7.

Action Plan for Year Five

Spiritual

1.

2.

3.

Emotional

1.

2.

3.

Family

1.

2.

3.

Career

1.

2.

3.

Physical

1.

2.

3.

Social

1.

2.

3.

Financial

1.

2.

3.

List Some of Your Roadblocks and Solutions

Obstacle:

1.

2.

3.

Solution:

1.

2.

3.

Obstacle:

1.

2.

3.

Solution:

1.

2.

3.

Obstacle:

1.

2.

3.

Solution:

1.

2.

3.

Obstacle:

1.

2.

3.

Solution:

1.

2.

3.

Achievements

This is where you list the things you achieved this year. Don't get discouraged if everything on your list wasn't accomplished; simply carry them over to the next year. Way to go!

This is to certify that I, _____, accomplished the following during year five_____:

1.

2.

3.

4.

5.

6.

7.

Transcendent Principles

You have heard me mention transcendent principles all throughout this book, and I am sure you are interesting in knowing what they are:

- Transcendent principle is the process of living supernaturally in all areas of our lives. These principles have been put to use by the greatest women ever to grace this earth.

- Transcendent principles will show you how to live your authentic life. It is the power to unlocking your dreams.

- Transcendent principles will release you from average to *fantastic*. The problem why depression is so extensive is partially due to women not experiencing extraordinary events in their lives.

- Transcendent principles will help you take care of emotional upheavals, sporadic attachments, and displacement issues.

- Transcendent principles will unlock your transitory mindset. You will move from incompletes to completions.

- Transcendent principles will bring you a world of new opportunities. You will suddenly find yourselves receiving offers that have eluded you in the past.

- Transcendent principles will make you a powerful woman, thereby giving those around you the audacity to shine.

- Transcendent principles will make you more attractive to others and attract influential and beautiful people to your life.

- Transcendent principles will show you how to tap into the under-utilized resources of your life.

- Transcendent principles will help you figure out how your geographical and generational positions influence your decisions.

- Transcendent principles will give you a spiritual principle that will change your life forever—literally!

- Transcendent principles will give you the power to help your children live balanced lives, make good friends, get into college of choice, become more spiritual, and even help you get along with your teenage children.

- Transcendent principles can change your life. By giving you more choices, more alternatives in the way you perceive yourself, live your life, and face your future.

Ask: What Can I Do to Help?

It's been a season for the world—hurricanes, tsunamis, earthquakes, famines, wars, foreclosures, economic depression, etc. Some of us are asking ourselves: What can I do to help? It is a time when donating money feels insufficient, and if you're like me, I simply want to go over there to help.

So why am I sending you this invitation that is going out to women everywhere? Well, because I have a mandate to require you to step into your authentic Life today. Seventy-five to eighty percent of Americans consider themselves Christians, and more consider themselves simply spiritual. But when you question them further, most believe that Christianity has no influence in their lives or communities.

I am seeking a group of women who are tired of trying to make things work from the mental or physical realm while losing all the backings or powers of the spiritual. These are usually women who get things done and can't contemplate having one more thing to their list.

There are many reasons why most people never achieve a level of skill beyond competence. One good one: Competence is usually good enough. It's usually enough to keep your job, to earn a decent living, and to enjoy the respect of your colleagues. But achieving competence is not enough if you want to do something extraordinary with your life. If you want to be more than just good, if you'd like to be great in at least one thing, then you have to be prepared to do what it takes to master a skill.

And what does it take?

My message is counter-culture because I say, *you can be extraordinary*! Don't buy into the gospel of downsizing your life. Our time on this planet is short; make your impact now!

You are part of this call to significance. Some of you are on your way to the top of the corporate ladder while others of you are just starting out. What we all have in common is the expectation of something better: knowing that there is a greater need that we get to fulfill.

We have created *The Center of Refuge*, an oasis for women who need a place to be rejuvenated and energized for action. So, I am seeking a group of women who want to change the world together. There is strength in numbers. My job is to demonstrate the transcendent principles that will invariably stimulate you to success. I'm expecting tremendous responses from this already dynamic group of women. Become a part of something *life changing*.

Weapons Released

I will be releasing these powerful prayers, so please, if you have a handkerchief or anointing oil or a piece of cloth, use them as a point of contact as you pray this prayer. Then use the oil on yourself or send to the person you prayed for. Let the windows of heaven open up to receive your requests. I pray that you are all strengthened with might in your inner minds and that Christ dwells richly on the inside of you. I release the power of God's favor to all those in need today.

I pray healing into the lives of all those that require healing. Healing is the children's bread so receive what belongs to you. May the power of his spirit saturate your homes and bodies.

Devil, the LORD rebukes you in Jesus's name. Take your hands off all that belongs to us in the name of Jesus. I breathe life into all dry bones today. Rise up from your sick beds and live a victorious life in Jesus's name.

LORD, restore broken marriages in your name. You said a three-fold cord is not easy broken so strengthen what's left of these marriages. Turn the hearts of the husbands and wives back to each other. Infuse them with new love for each other so your name is glorified.

I pray for those that have been tormented and hurt emotionally. Release them from turmoil today. There are those who have been abused, lost children, or loved ones. Lead them besides the still waters so their souls might be refreshed. Grant them the wisdom to release all the hurt and pains as you give them a new lease on life. Let today become the first day of their peace.

Receive the wisdom to be spiritual parents who raise spiritual children. Our children are for signs and wonders, so I command all spirits of adversity away from them in Jesus's name. They will excel in their land. They will stand up for the truth. They will champion the cause of the poor. They will prosper in all that they do. They will become a mighty army to be used by the power of God. No evil will interrupt their destiny. They are hidden in the palm of the Most High God. We snatch our children way from jaws of hell and set them on the path of grace. All children and grandchildren that have gone astray will return to their homes in Jesus's name, amen.

Thank you for sending your angels to all troubled parts of the world. Thanks for helping people to safety and releasing the captives. Continue to do a glorious work in our midst in Jesus's name.

Experience joy and peace. Become immense in your destiny. Be restored to your source. Since everything in nature settles into its own space, I declare that you will be settled in your place. You will no longer struggle to flourish as a human being. Your beauty will shine, and the glory inside you will glow in Jesus's name. Amen.

We pray for this country, O God, still the hands of the avenger. We are asking for your mercy and not judgment. We confess our sins and pray that you forgive us and lead your people back to your once again. We are tired of the dysfunction in this society, so as a mighty army, we let out a loud shout of *peace*!

Post Script

You will become successful because you have laid the foundation for a successful life. My definitions of success are posted on my office wall: "Success is the freedom to live the life of destiny," and "Success is freedom to fulfill your purpose." Both definitions tell me that you cannot live the life of purpose if you are weighed down with mundane stuff. If you don't have money to pay your electricity bill, how can you live a purposeful life? How can you live a purposeful life if you are being tossed in the winds of financial difficulties, family issues, career, and educational problems? You cannot become a success until you fight your way out of the life's mediocrities. If you're having problem attaining any of your goals, get help, do it well, and get on with life.

Human beings are created for success. Once you accept the possibility of succeeding within your world, the rest becomes easy. Believing the possibility of your success changes your life. Your conversations will be different; you might behave differently, and dress differently as you pursue your goals.

Your nature doesn't want you to become a failure. Its deepest cry is to rise above adversity and mediocrity. It takes more work to be a loser than to become a winner.

Losing works against your nature. If you would just follow that inner desire, you will become a winner.

A successful person is someone who is aligned with destiny. Successful persons are in tune with their winning nature. Nobody was born a loser. We all begin life with everything we need to succeed. You already have within you all of the ingredients needed for you to successfully rise above your circumstances. Failure is not an option. Live your desires!

> *A Lived Desire*
>
> Desires
> Deeper hopes and dreams
> Grazing within my soul
> Living in places unfurled
> Longing for release
> In surrender
> I find my way home
> A life designed
> For greatness and grace
> I discover passion on the road
> To the Serengeti
> Danced the night in the galaxy of Adonai
> Parted the river Jordan and drank of the new wine
> I discovered the universe works for me
> Substances billow
> With sacrifices climbing the hill
> My ram is caught waiting for slaughter
> Night sweats; angels appear
> The wrestle is complete
> Jacob has surrendered
> My limp is indication that I triumph

Soul Desires

and I'm endowed with strength
With blessing of the breasts
And of heavens above
Now life is complete with abundance
My table of dreams
Dine with me!

Merino, 2011.

Appendix

Praise Outline

- Lord, you are so good to me
- Who is like my God among the earth
- You are the one who speaks, and the earth trembles
- You are God all by yourself
- You are the Ancient of Days
- The Ageless One
- The all powerful and almighty
- You are the source of all joy and power
- You are the miracle worker
- You are the way maker
- You are the God of breakthrough who makes a way where there is no way

- You are glorious and wonderful
- Full of goodness and mercy
- The horn of my salvation
- The way, the truth, and my life and my salvation
- You are the God of justice and mercy
- Righteousness and truth are the foundation of your throne
- I come before your throne of grace by the blood of Jesus
- I honor you; I hallow your name
- You are good to me; you are kind;
- Your steadfast love is new every morning
- You are my light and source of inspiration
- You are God all by yourself
- You have purposed and will bring it to pass
- Let everyone be a liar and you remain faithful
- You fill the heavens and Earth with your glory and majesty
- I stand in awe of you
- You are glorious in holiness and fearful in praises

- You are the creator; you make everything beautiful in your time
- You are Adonai, the merciful and gracious God
- You are Jehovah, the God who makes everything right
- Righteousness and truth are the foundation of your throne
- You see me when no one else seems to care
- You made me in your own special way, and I am glad to call you Father
- You made me with care and thoughtfulness; how marvelous are your thoughts
- toward me.
- I love you LORD, and I call you Father
- My LORD and King
- The beautiful One
- The Only wise God
- The Greatest; the Almighty; The Omniscient, and Transcendent
- I call you Holy!
- I call you righteous!
- I call you Father!

- I call you Mother!
- I call you Husband!
- I call you my Friend!
- I call you Mighty!
- I call you All Powerful!
- I call you Giver!
- I call you Healer!
- I call you Wonder!
- I call you Savior!
- I call you Spirit!
- I call you Way-Maker!
- I call you Seer!
- I call you Master!
- I call you Teacher!
- I call you Leader!
- I call you Lord!
- I call you Helper!
- I call you life Giver!
- I call you my joy, my peace, my hope, and my faith.

Soul Desires

- I call you Love!
- I call you Light!
- I call you Word!
- I call you Freedom!
- I call you my God!
- You are my praise
- you are my song
- You are the glory and lifter of my head
- You are my hiding place
- You are my rock
- You are my redeemer
- You are my provider
- You are my Ebenezer
- You are my strength
- You are my life
- You are my wheel within the wheel
- You are my shining star
- You are my atonement
- You are next breath

- You are Abraham's covenant keeping God
- You are Isaac's reward
- You are Jacob's second chance
- You are Joseph's dream
- You are Moses's rod
- You are Israel's "I Am"
- You are Miriam's song
- You are Joshua's army
- You are Rahab's deliverer
- You are the Ruth kinsman redeemer
- You are Samuel's prophecy
- You are David's friend
- You are Solomon's wisdom
- You are Elijah's fire
- You are Ezra's restorer of the temple
- You are Nehemiah's rebuilder of broken down walls of human life
- You are Esther's scepter
- You are Job's hedge of protection
- You are Isaiah's "who shall I send?"

SOUL DESIRES

- You are Jeremiah's lamentation
- You are Ezekiel's wheel in the middle of a wheel
- You are Daniel's fourth man in life's fiery furnace
- You are Hosea's restorer of women's dignity
- You are Joel's trumpet in Zion
- You are Amos's call to repentance
- You are Obadiah's holiness
- You are Jonah's obedience
- You are Micah' mountain of the LORD's house
- You are Nahum's destruction
- You are Habakkuk's vision
- You are Zephaniah's judgment of nations
- You are Haggai's wealth
- You are Zechariah's city without walls
- You are Malachi's tithe
- You are Matthew's Messiah
- You are Mark's cross
- You are Luke's physician
- You are John's love

- You are Acts of the church
- You are Roman's grace
- You are Corinthian's gifts
- You are Galatian's redeemer
- You are Ephesian's Head of the Church
- You are Phillipian's supplier of needs
- You are Colossian's image of the Father
- You are Thessalonian's "Soon coming King"
- You are Timothy's Day Star
- You are Titus's doctrine
- You are Philemon's mentor
- You are Hebrew's faith
- You are James's practice
- You are Peter's divine nature
- You are John's prosperity
- You are Jude's warning
- You are Revelation's Judge and King

Restoration Scriptures

- Psalm 51:12 "Restore to me the joy of your salvation and grant me a willing spirit, to sustain me."

- Joel 2:25 "I will restore to you the years that the locust has eaten…"

- Isaiah 53:3-5 "He is despised and rejected by men, a Man of sorrows and acquainted with grief… Surely He has borne our grief and carried our sorrows; yet we esteemed him stricken, smitten by God and afflicted. He was wounded for our transgression, and bruised for our iniquities; the chastisement for our peace was upon Him and by His stripes we are healed.

- Ezekiel 16:6 "When I passed by you and saw you squirming in your blood, I said to you while you were in your blood, 'Live!' Yes, I said to you while you were in your blood, 'Live!'

- Isaiah 50:7 "for the Lord God will help me; therefore I will not be disgraced.

- Isaiah 49:25 "…but I will contend with him who contends with you and I will save your children

- Isaiah 49:19 "Can a woman forget her nursing child and not have compassion on the son of her womb? Surely they may forget. Yet I will not forget you. See, I have inscribed you on the palm of my hands; your walls are continually before me.

- Jeremiah 15:18 "why is my pain perpetual and my wound incurable, which refuses to be healed?

- Psalm 147:3 "He heals the brokenhearted and binds up their wounds."

- John 10:10 "The thief comes only to steal and kill and destroy; I have come that they may have life, and have it to the full."

- Hebrews 4:16 "Let us then approach the throne of grace with confidence, so that we may receive mercy and find grace to help us in our time of need."

- Philippians 4:6-7 "Do not be anxious about anything, but in everything, by prayer and petition, with thanksgiving, present your requests to God. And the peace of God, which transcends all understanding, will guard your hearts and your minds in Christ Jesus."

Two Hundred *I Ams*

I am beautifully and wonderfully created.
I am positively ravishing.
I am radiant.
I am a sweet wife/husband.
I am a loving wife/husband.
I am successful.
I am wealthy beyond imagination.
I am confident.
I am admired.
I am beautiful.
I am delightful.
I am free to excel.
I am positive.
I am brilliant.
I am at peace.
I am stress free.
I am wonderful.
I am present.
I am loving.
I am patient.
I am a fountain of joy.
I am sexy.
I am a fantastic lover.
I am my beloved.
I am a wall, and my breast like towers.
I am prosperous.
I am charismatic.
I am honest.
I am still.
I am gentle.
I am kind.
I am meek.
I am strong.
I am admirable.
I am creative.
I am sufficient.
I am healthy.
I am blessed.
I am healed.
I am free of guilt.
I am forgiven.
I am a lover.
I am a forgiver.
I am patient.
I am free of profanity.
I am articulate.

I am composed.
I am at peace.
I am joyful.
I am happy.
I am satisfied.
I am patient.
I am experiencing success.
I am courageous.
I am personable.
I am suitable.
I am good enough.
I am an overcomer.
I am reflective.
I have all I need now.
I like myself.
I love living.
I forgive myself.
I release anger.
I am a good listener.
I am accepted.
I am accepting of others.
I receive love.
I show love.
I am free of shame.
I am fit.
I am sharing.
I am losing weight.
I am efficient and organized.
I am considerate of others.
I am cognizant of my limitations.
I am honest and truthful.
I radiate charm.
I am fearless.
I am a winner.
I am the head and never the tail.
I am blessed in my going out and coming in.
I have reproducing power.
I am a creative force.
I am safe.
I am rich.
I am obedient.
I am being transformed.
I am a leader.
I am a promoter.
I am analytical.
I am a helper.
I am a prince.
I am a princess.
I am royalty.
I am a queen.
I am abundant.
I am nourished.

I am nurturing.
I am the most influential person in my life.
I am an excellent student.
I excel at work.
I have a flourishing business.
I am promoted.
I have more understanding than all my teachers.
I have favor.
I am fun to be with.
I chose good friends.
I have all that I need.
I like myself.
I fit in.
I am sober.
I am nicotine-free.
I am alcohol-free.
I am cholesterol-free.
I am sugar-free.
I live a balanced life.
I eat moderately.
I am educated.
I am literate.
I travel around the world.
I feel affectionate toward…
I have multiple orgasms with my loving husband.
I am able to network.
I make good friends.
I am proud of my body.
I see a beautiful woman.
I love my nose.
I admire my eyes.
I love my well-rounded hips.
I am turned-on by my spouse.
I treasure every moment.
I enjoy my children.
I listen without passing judgments.
I create winning situations.
I participate fully.
I am fully involved.
I am daily seeking perfection.
I owe nothing.
I am free.
I am enlightened.
I am gorgeous.
I see the good in mankind.

I love my family.
I have everything
I need to create
my happiness.
I am hired.
I am favored.
I am accepted.
I have beautiful lips.
I meditate.
I give to others.
I rejoice in goodness.
I am full of hope.
I am full of faith.
I am faithful to
my spouse.
I am inspired.
My mind is clear
and alert.
I receive wisdom.
I am fully invested
in my life.
I am fertile.
I am pregnant.
I am filled with…
I am interesting.
I am complex.
I am communicating.
I am adventurous.
I am nice.
I am a living desire.
I have my living desires.
I am fully involved in
the world.
I help the children.
I believe in innocence.
I fight for justice.
I fight for peace.
I help the less fortunate.
I help myself.
I receive assistance.
I am overjoyed.
I am complete.
I am an instrument
of peace.
I am a child.
I am a mother.
I fully participate.
I am faithful.
I am overjoyed.
I am calm.
I am contributing to
my world.
I am a source of light
in my world.
I am benevolent.
I am respectful.
I am accommodating.
I am opened to new
ways,
ideas, and thoughts.
I am a visionary.
I am expanding

Soul Desires

my horizon.
I am committed
to excellence.
I am free of bitterness.

I am a willing
participant in my life.
I am intuitive.

REFERENCES

1. How to Create & Fill Out My Family Genogram Map. Retieved from eHow.com http://www.ehow.com/how_6134799_create-out-family-genogram-map.html#ixzz1Rf7NUYcw

2. Maslow. Retrieved from http://honolulu.hawaii.edu/intranet/committees/FacDevCom/guidebk/teachtip/maslow.htm

3. Depression. Retrieved from http://www.drpodell.org/alternative_treatments_for_depression.shtmlhttp://www.seattlehealingarts.com/therapies_more.htm#neuro1

4. Marc Galanter, M.D. (2008). Spirituality, Evidence-Based Medicine, and Alcoholics Anonymous Am J Psychiatry 165:1514-1517 doi:10.1176/appi.ajp.2008.08050678

5. James W: The Varieties of Religious Experience (1902). New York, Modern Library, 1936.

6. Kessler RC, Soukup J, Davis RB, Foster DF, Wilkey SA, Van Rompay MI, Eisenberg DM: The use of

complementary and alternative therapies to treat anxiety and depression in the United States. Am J Psychiatry 2001; 158:289–294]

7. Koenig, H. McCullough M, & Larson D. (2001). *Handbook of Religion and Health*. Oxford: Oxford University Press

8. Culliford, L. (2002) Spiritual Care and Psychiatric Treatment: An Introduction. *Advances in Psychiatric Treatment*, 8, 249-261

9. Greasley, P., Chiu, L.F., & Gartland, Rev. M. (2001) The concept of spiritual care in mental health nursing. *Journal of Advanced Nursing*, 33 (5), 629-637

10. Culliford, L. (2002); Greasley, P., Chiu, L.F., & Gartland, Rev. M. (2001)

11. World Health Organization. (1998) WHOQOL and Spirituality, Religiousness and Personal Beliefs: Report on WHO Consultation. Geneva: WHO

12. Ellis A. Psychotherapy and atheistic values: a response to A. E. Bergin's "Psychotherapy and religious values." *J Consult Clin Psychol.* 1980; 48:635-639.